Commuter's Tale

JONATHAN MARGOLIS, 37, is a former London bus conductor, number N119481, a veteran of routes 86 (Romford to Limehouse) and 193 (Hornchurch to Ilford). He is now the TV critic for the *Mail on Sunday* and also writes for *Time* Magazine. He wrote *Cleese Encounters*, the best-selling biography of John Cleese. He has commuted extensively, on the number 29 bus in Leeds, the 5A in Nottingham, as well as the Central and District Lines on London's Tube. When in New York, he commutes on foot. He lives in West London.

GABRIELLE MORRIS, 23, an English graduate from London University, is a freelance writer. Her work has appeared in the *Guardian*, the *Mail on Sunday*, the *Yorkshire Post* and the *Modern Review*. Paradoxically, she has a strong aversion to all forms of public transport and lives in Lancashire, where she is saving up to buy her own train.

The Commuter's Tale

Jonathan Margolis and
Gabrielle Morris

Illustrations by David Gaskill

CHAPMANS

Chapmans Publishers Ltd
141–143 Drury Lane
London WC2B 5TB

First published by Chapmans 1992
Selection and editorial matter
© Jonathan Margolis and Gabrielle Morris 1992
© in the illustrations David Gaskill 1992

ISBN 1 85592 631 8

A CIP catalogue record for this book is available from
the British Library

Typeset by MC Typeset Ltd,
Wouldham, Rochester, Kent.
Printed and bound in Great Britain

For A. Spokesman, who will continue to be 'looking into it' for centuries to come. For BR staff in Manchester, who call their trains 'Scuds' – because they often fail to reach their destination. And for the New York commuter who filed a suit for over $1 million in damages for the mental anguish caused by travelling on the railway, claiming that the appalling service was driving him crazy.

Preface

Sex and money are the two subjects about which nobody, anywhere ever tells the truth, 'I love you' and 'The cheque's in the post' being the other great universal lies.

But there is another statement, made every day, that is equally and unerringly fallacious.

This eternal untruth takes a variety of forms, but always amounts to the same – lying about how long it takes to get to and from work.

We will boast that it takes 15 minutes door-to-door to impress upon people how clever we were choosing to live in a particular place.

On the same day, we will moan that it takes two hours, as a way of showing how unfair life has been to us.

A commuter is someone who does not go along one bit with Robert Louis Stevenson's idea that 'To travel hopefully is a better thing than to arrive'. He or she who wrestles daily with the Bakerloo Line, the Ginza Line, the Long Island Railroad or the M25 is more than happy to arrive and forget all about the travelling.

It is one of the tragedies of the modern world, albeit one that has given us a good few laughs during the research for this book, that commuters don't always arrive quite as they hope to.

Commuting is one of the most fertile areas for apocrypha, urban mythology, deceit and one-upmanship – along with genuine but preposterous stories – that life offers.

Yet at the same time it unites most of the adult working population, who have come to resemble a horde of obsessively indecisive lemmings. By morning they swarm insanely one way, and the same evening, as if they have changed their mind, stampede back along their own tracks. Repeat the performance a few thousand times, and they can retire.

A survey by a Japanese insurance company in 1991 revealed that more than 7 people are crushed into 1 square metre of space on some of Tokyo's rush-hour trains. It also calculated that the average office worker on a 5-day working week spent more than 2 years of his life travelling in these conditions.

Kotsu senso – commuting war – is an international phenomenon. Len Crawford of Dartford, a commuter of 15 years' standing, never commuted on the Tokyo subway or fought his way through the crowds at Shinjuku station, but he could have done so easily if asked.

Mr Crawford gave his advice to *London Evening News* readers in 1972. It included such wisdom as sitting down as soon as the train heaved into Cannon Street to let fellow passengers clear the train as he relaxed for five minutes.

He went on to outline more of his philosophy of getting to work: 'Travelling on the train is the hardest part of the day. This is what I get paid for. Working in the office is a relaxation period, a breathing space to prepare you for the journey home.' His particular technique, he added, was 'To shut my eyes and think of Majorca.'

Mr Donald Gallop, the less-than-aptly named station

manager, commented: 'It's a shame new commuters cannot undergo a course of instruction. It's a pleasure to watch an experienced commuter in action.'

Few officials are as impressed by commuters as Mr Gallop was by Mr Crawford. Superintendent Steve Chapman of the British Transport Police was none too complimentary when he let rip once at the average British commuter. 'Talk about Jekyll and Hyde', he said of peak-time travellers. 'Perfectly nice people normally, I'm sure. But between work and home, they are out of the traps like long dogs – heads down, blinkers on, elbows out. And whenever one of them goes down – tripped up, maybe, or even seriously assaulted – they just step over the body and away.' Warming to his subject, Steve continued: 'They treat BR staff badly enough, but even my officers get sworn at, spat at, poked with umbrellas, smashed out of the way. Ten minutes later, and there they are again, rocking gently in their seats on the train home: pale, perspiring, still a bit fish-faced but model British citizens once more – orderly, quiet, conducting themselves as perfect strangers, each man an island of magnificently battened-down stress.'

BR's Southern Region once attacked commuters for not being on time for their trains. A survey they undertook purported to prove that half their 300,000 customers left home too late. A spokesman crowed: 'If all our trains arrived in London on time, more than 150,000 people would still be late for work every day.'

But generally, BR takes a gritty 'the-customer-is-always-right' approach, or blames late trains on the familiar problems – incorrect snow, leaves on the line, or in one splendid case, when an entire barn roof landed on the tracks in Sussex, eaves on the line.

The role of the poor transport system spokesman is that of official patsy, with the job of commenting on the uncommentable-upon, such as when a 1980 report by a sex therapist in Winchester blamed British Rail and the strain of commuting on a nasty outbreak of impotency in the town. Asked to comment, the spokesman predictably denied that BR were marriage-wreckers: 'I don't think this is a problem isolated to trains,' he wailed. 'It probably applies to other types of travel as well.'

Another spokesman was left to clean up the mess after Bob Brakewell, divisional director for BR's West Anglia region, blew his top at a meeting with commuters on the Cambridge line who complained about their trains. 'If you're so dissatisfied with the service,' steamed Mr Brakewell, 'why don't you club together and buy your own train and we'll run it for you? They only cost £2.5 million each.' A spokesman clarified: 'He said it in a light-hearted way.'

Alongside the friends who have told us their favourite commuting stories, we are indebted to hundreds of newspapers around the world for the loving detail and relish with which they tell their local commuters' tales. Not all the best stories originated on the M25 or Network SouthEast. Commuting hells from Yokohama to Bombay have been equally rich pastures for us to feed in.

The Commuting Cockup
as an Art Form

THE HISTORY OF commuting is the history of the cockup. Wherever man and 8.10 come together – or more likely don't – the possibility of ineptitude, misunderstanding and plain bad luck hangs deliciously in the air. When you study the commuting debacle as we have, it begins to seem almost a miracle that anyone, anywhere in the world, has ever got to work, let alone made it to the office *and* back. Selecting our favourite commuting disaster has been a joyously painful experience. The story we begin with, and we feel sets the tone for this catalogue of catastrophe, was told us by the former *Daily Telegraph* journalist Henry Miller, who now lives in the USA. Given the status of the *Daily Telegraph* as the British commuter's bible (as well as his makeshift umbrella, thing for rolling up and poking ticket inspectors with and so on), it is fitting that the following happened to a journalist on the newspaper. His name was Norman Riley, and it happened to him in the early 1960s.

Mr Riley lived in Sussex, where he raised pigs, and one evening managed to sneak away from the *Telegraph*'s Fleet Street office relatively early so that he could get home to tend his animals. He phoned his wife and asked her if she would be so kind as to meet the 6 p.m. train from Waterloo. When he got to Waterloo, a good 15 minutes before the train was due to leave, Mr Riley went

3

for a drink at the station bar. There he met an old Fleet Street friend he hadn't seen since the war.

Needless to say, Mr Riley missed his train. He phoned his wife in Sussex to ask her to meet the next train, but by now, she had already left for the rural station. Seeing he was not on the train, she stormed back home, just in time for Mr Riley's next anguished call. This time, he promised, he would be on the 6.45, in the third carriage, and please, please could she meet him? She set off for the station again.

Sure enough, Mr Riley was there, in the third carriage – as his wife observed when the train, a non-stop to the South Coast as it turned out – sped through the station. Mrs Riley set off home yet again, a 12-mile drive, and arrived just in time for Mr Riley's third phone call – this time from Brighton, where he had ended up. Yes, he would be in the third carriage again. Yes, he was dreadfully, dreadfully sorry.

And yes, the 8.20 from Brighton to Waterloo once again steamed through Mr Riley's home station without so much as slowing down. Four and a half hours after he left the office to get home early, Mr Riley was back where he started, in the bar at Waterloo station, drowning what were now quite considerable sorrows.

. . .

In 1981, British Rail launched a scheme for the disabled. At Euston the scene was set for the great opening. Peter Parker, the Chairman of BR, was present, and a gold-suited Jimmy Savile, pushing Mrs Audrey Thompson's wheelchair, was ready to board the train.

Unfortunately the chair got stuck. 'It very nearly did it,' came the rueful comment from BR, 'but one arm of the chair got in the way. We could have got it through the door all right, but not past the seat and into the compartment.'

The cause of the problem was simple. BR had designed the 875 coaches on the advice that the standard wheelchair is 24 inches wide.

It is, but not when there's somebody sitting in it, whereupon it expands. An embarrassed BR said that it would look into making adjustments.

. . .

John Honeysett and his bride Sarah spent weeks in the summer of 1991 organizing their wedding. They arranged for all their guests, with hats and bouquets at the ready, to be on a Portsmouth to Cardiff train, which would then make an unscheduled stop at the village of Netley in Hampshire to pick up the newlyweds. They would then travel on to Bath on the first part of a honeymoon trip to Dublin. To nobody's enormous surprise, the meticulously organized wedding went awry, the train with guests on board charging through Netley without so much as slowing down. The newlyweds were stranded. John and Sarah were especially upset; he works as a railway booking clerk, while her father was a BR driver.

. . .

Antonio Riccio was intent upon being honourable but in the end he only succeeded in paralysing a railway network and being interrogated by the police.

It started when Antonio, a 26-year-old furniture salesman, bought £1,300 worth of goods in Northern Italy and paid by cheque. Knowing that he didn't have that much in his account, he expected to pick up some extra cash in Rome and have paid it into his account in Naples before the cheque came through.

He collected the money from Rome without a hitch, but then the trouble began. Due to a rail dispute there was only one daily train running south to Naples. Antonio caught it, thinking that it would stop in his home town. It did not. Panic-stricken, Antonio pulled the communication cord, leapt out and headed for the bank. But the police saw him, thought he was a 'mad bomber' and arrested him. When they heard his story they allowed him to get to the bank in time. The following week he was found guilty of stopping the train without good reason and fined £7. Antonio, always an honourable man, paid the fine on the spot.

. . .

The M25, being circular, is an incomparable laboratory for *aficionados* of the commuting cock-up. Bob Fleming's experience on the road in 1991 was a classic. He set out from Hoo in Kent at 5 a.m. to drive to Durham, 325 miles away. Ten hours later, when he was stopped by police for driving too slowly, he discovered that he was only 15 miles from home.

To make things more confusing, the PC who stopped him was himself from Durham. Recognizing the accent with relief, Mr Fleming asked 'How far to Durham?' When he was told he was still in Kent, he assumed the PC was having him on. In the ten hours he had been on the road, Mr Fleming had lapped the M25 four times. PC Batey, who had stopped Mr Fleming for driving too slowly and erratically, said: 'He was shell-shocked, he was on his own in a Cortina and he had set off 10 hours before.'

When Mr Fleming realized what he had done he told the police: 'I'm going home. I'll try again tomorrow.'

.   .   .

A biker who got lost on the M25 took two days to find his way home. Retired dustman George Til-burt, aged 49, started the half-hour journey from his sister's in Basingstoke to his home in Wey-bridge, Surrey, on his Honda.

Becoming hopelessly confused on the ring-road, he spent the next couple of days shooting off slip-roads which took him all over the Home Counties on the M1, M11 and M4.

George only stopped his tour because he ran out of fuel. Once stopped, he parked on the hard shoulder and rang the police. When they arrived, they gave him a couple of gallons of petrol and 'nursed' him home by giving him directions and alerting colleagues to watch his progress. Once home, George vowed: 'Next time, I'm taking the train.'

. . .

Next on were Roy and Joy Kinsley-Poynter, who on Good Friday 1991 left Southampton in their trusty Lada and headed up to Scotland to see their dream home. They had withdrawn £4,000 for a deposit on the perfect retirement home, just 20 miles outside Edinburgh.

Preparing for such a long journey, they packed the car with everything they thought they would need – except the map.

After 1,503 miles, mainly driving in circles, the couple conceded that leaving the map behind 'was probably a mistake'.

Mrs Kinsley-Poynter, 69, did most of the driving, while her husband, 76, who does not drive himself, did his best to navigate.

The first problem arose at Birmingham where the couple spent hours circling Kidderminster. Finally discovering their mistake, they continued north. Once across the border, they missed the

Edinburgh turn-off, hit Aberdeen and spent 21 hours touring the Grampians.

Exhausted, they finally arrived at their farmhouse destination and decided that it was truly lovely. But after just half an hour they set off for home.

They reached home on Thursday after a similarly diverse route. Nursing swollen legs from a week in the passenger seat, Mr Kinsley-Poynter said: 'We must have seen Kidderminster at least 25 times. We thought we knew the way but I suppose we didn't. We were a bit cocky.'

For the first couple of days, the couple did not stop to eat. Mr Kinsley-Poynter said: 'We were in a bit of a hurry and only had a piece of bread and butter in the car.'

His wife admitted that the journey had been conducted at an average of 10 m.p.h. with an increase to 35 m.p.h. on the motorway. 'Quite fast enough,' said Mr Kinsley-Poynter. 'It should be the national speed limit.'

Unfortunately lorry drivers caught behind their Lada didn't agree with them, and Mr Kinsley-Poynter admitted that some of the Lada's mileage had been clocked up on what he described as 'that hard pad along the side of the road'.

The couple, who had wanted to move in order to avoid the congestion they believed the Channel Tunnel would bring to the South, have now abandoned their plans. Mr Kinsley-Poynter said: 'The house was beautiful, but I'm afraid we won't be able to buy it. We'd never last another trip.'

A group of day-trippers returning from France were treated to a scenic lap of the M25 by their confused coach driver. And in case they had missed some of the more aesthetic aspects of the gargantuan ring-road the first time round, he did another lap.

Having missed the M1 exit, the bemused driver didn't bother turning back at the next exit, but kept going, thus covering an extra 124 miles. He didn't stop until he got back to the A2, where he had first joined London's orbital road from Dover. Having to refuel, he asked a policeman for directions before driving back to the M1 exit.

The party eventually arrived home in Leicester four hours late at 6.30 a.m. One of the passengers, Glen Evans, said, 'We told the driver what he had done, but his eyes were glued on the road and he said he'd sort it out. We seemed to be driving for ever.'

. . .

Grandfather William Allen, aged 84, broke the record for time spent on the M25 when he went to visit his daughter in the South. His journey was dogged somewhat by the fact he had left his address book at home and only remembered that his daughter lived near an airport in a place beginning with 'R'.

A motorist found Mr Allen in a confused state parked in a lay-by on the M25 and called the police. Mr Allen was taken to the police station where it transpired that he had spent approximately two days on the M25 trying to find his daughter's home.

He had left home at 7 a.m., but his daughter Joan didn't see him until 2 a.m. two days later. Mr Allen had been looking for Reigate, near Gatwick, when he should have been looking for Ruislip, near Heathrow.

Mr Allen said he wasn't sure exactly how many circuits he had done, but remembered that he had driven through a tunnel several times. Joan said her father was thoroughly embarrassed by the whole episode but had set off back home in his car.

. . .

Even criminals forget that successful commuting is a vital part of any career. In 1991, a plot to steal Van Gogh paintings worth £130 million was scotched when the raiders found during their final pre-raid check that their getaway car had been clamped. None of the trio had enough money to have it removed, so they resorted to attempting to dislodge it themselves. Three men were apprehended by the police as they jacked up the car, which had been parked on double yellow lines – brilliant touch, that – in Soho Square.

The trio were found to be carrying firearms, explosives, a Browning blank-firing self-loading pistol, a telescopic cosh, a survival knife, a butterfly knife and two hand grenades. Police searching the car also found a sledgehammer, a crowbar and, in case anybody should be under any mis-apprehension about their aim, a plan of the gallery with a mark by the room containing the Van Goghs – the initials VG. The three denied attempting to steal a number of paintings from the National Gallery.

The failed raiders were doubly unlucky. It was an ideal time for burglary at the gallery as security was being revamped. This meant that there was no internal alarm system, no video cameras and only two warders on guard in the rear foyer.

The prosecution compared the trio's efforts to the farcical style of one of Peter Sellers' Pink Panther films. One of the triumvirate had been so sure of a successful mission that he had already consulted a copy of *Who's Who*, 'borrowed' from a Sussex library, which lists well-known art dealers who might have been interested in relieving him of his haul. Along with a friend, he had also taken the trouble to attend a number of art classes.

The extent of the confidence of the would-be raiders was revealed by the cheques found at one of their homes. One was written to Harrods for £33,000, one to Lloyds Insurance for £2,000 and the third to Lamborghini for £60,000.

They were joined on the roll of honour in 1992 by two Irish burglars, who, leaving the scene of their hitherto successful crime, discovered that their getaway driver had fled. So Patrick Docherty, 47, and his brother Sean, 40, stopped the first motorist that they saw. It was a police car. The gentleman inside was only too pleased to help them.

But no one in this line could touch Tony Alivia for hubris. This Milanese criminal parked his getaway car in a prominent position and then went off to rob a bank. After a perfectly satisfactory raid, Alivia sped back to his car only to find that it was not there. A thief had stolen it.

Police found a shocked Alivia staring at the spot where his car ought to have been. As they hand-cuffed him, he was heard to complain 'You can't trust anyone these days. There are too many thieves about.'

· · ·

Robin Bennett, a young man from London, had a touch of bad luck with his car. Coming off the M4 in 1992, he was rammed by two girls in an expensive Citroën. Driving on to the nearest con-venient stop, both parties stopped in a bus shelter to assess the damage.

Uppermost in Mr Bennett's mind at that mo-ment was that his insurance had run out at mid-night the night before. Therefore much to the surprise of the apologetic young ladies, he made light of his broken back bumper and suggested that since no real harm had been done they should call it quits rather than wait for the boring business of getting the insurance people to sort out the mess.

The girls couldn't believe their luck and went grinning back to their car. Mr Bennett, also not believing his luck, went grinning back to his. But as he approached his vehicle, a double-decker bus pulled into the bus stop and took his car door off. Now, he was liable for several hundred pounds' worth of mashed bus panelling and a heavy fine for not being insured.

He hooked the door back onto its hinges, pushed the wires and springs back into place so that he could partially close the door, and slowly made his way home. The following Monday he sold the car for scrap.

. . .

A woman in Oldham drove up a cul-de-sac by mistake. Panicking, she went down a subway into a pedestrian-only shopping precinct, then down another subway and onto the road she was seeking – after weaving in and out of some handily placed trees.

. . .

Teacher Pat Sharp was arrested in front of 200 pupils after a moment of commuting forgetfulness. The nightmare began when Mr Sharp couldn't remember where he had parked his car after a shopping trip.

He went to the police, who later checked with Mr Sharp's doctor about his suitability to drive. The doctor told police that Mr Sharp suffered from epilepsy. 'Rubbish,' said Mr Sharp. 'The only thing I have suffered from is diabetes, and I have driven safely for 20 years.'

The police informed the Driving and Vehicle Licensing Centre who sent him a message querying his medical history, and when he failed to reply they suspended his licence without his knowledge. Consequently he was arrested at his school for driving without a licence. 'It's incredible,' said Mr Sharp, 'I have had flu for a week and I was just confused about where I had parked the car.'

. . .

Caught in a 5-mile tail-back, the driver snoozed as a monster rush-hour traffic jam built up behind him – and, though he was unaware of it, cameras from national TV news filmed him.

Coming home from a business meeting, Chris, who refused to give his surname, was caught in traffic. 'I must have moved just 200 yards in half an hour. It was a warm evening and I must have dozed off. The next thing I knew, my car door was pulled open and the police were asking me if I was all right.' An even bigger jam had built up behind him and motorists were honking their horns.

Chris, a keen rally driver, was awarded the P.R. ATT of the Year award by his car club – a bedpan – on the strength of his achievement. A couple of days after the incident Chris was phoned by a traffic policeman who asked: 'Hello sir, are you awake now?'

. . .

In 1979, a safe-driving expert was fined £75 and banned for three months for – what else – dangerous driving. The 49-year-old had come sixth out of 20,000 entrants in a safe driving competition in Scotland. The Sheriff found him guilty of driving without due care and attention. The unfortunate's car hit the car of a garage proprietor who had stopped at a roundabout to attend to a breakdown. Mr Anderson, the Sheriff concluded, had been driving too close to the parked car. Our hero received his safe-driving award while awaiting trial.

Yet this case was not unique. Another driver told a magistrate in Cambridge that the reason he had made an illegal U-turn on the motorway was that he had missed his turn-off and was in a hurry. He explained that he didn't want to be late for the final session of the driver improvement course being run by the police.

. . .

George Simpson, 38, was a bit miffed when he finally got to work during a rail strike. He had just endured a miserable, crowded bus journey to get into his office in the centre of Birmingham from his home in Kings Norton. While congratulating himself on his achievement, he was told he needed his car for a business trip and would have to return home for it immediately.

. . .

Lovers of Spike Milligan should be grateful to a Southend taxi driver called Mr Moy. For one day Mr Moy picked up Mr Milligan's publisher, Jack Hobbs. When he delivered Mr Hobbs to his destination, Moy discovered that the publisher had unwittingly left behind the manuscript of the latest volume of Milligan's war memoirs. *Monty – His Part in my Victory* had taken Milligan three years to complete.

Hobbs spent a fretful evening contemplating the prospect of breaking the news to Milligan. Fortunately, Mr Moy traced Mr Hobbs and handed the manuscript over in one piece. A suitable tribute to Mr Moy was added when the book was published.

· · ·

An Irish company's fractionally downbeat launch of a new type of bus in 1980 was reported by Stephen Pile in one of his magnificent compendia of failures. The vehicle, touted as 'The bus of the Eighties', was to be driven out of the depot by the Irish Transport Minister. Sadly, when he tried to start the engine, the battery was flat. They replaced it. It still failed to start, so mechanics worked under the bus as the launch ceremony proceeded. The champagne bottle the minister hurled at the bus failed to break. When it did, it drenched the mayor of Limerick. A churchman blessed the bus when it finally started, but to no avail; it broke down half way to a reception in nearby Bunratty.

· · ·

In 1986, protesting Italian lorry drivers drove along non-motorway roads at 35 m.p.h. Their demonstration was over increased fines for speeding and dangerous driving, as well as the practice of confiscating vehicles as severe punishment.

But the go-slow achieved the opposite of the drivers' intentions, for instead of creating havoc, police reported that road traffic was normal. In fact in many areas the situation was better than on a routine working day.

.　.　.

Car windscreen cleaners at a junction in Padua caused havoc when they took it into their own hands to increase their earnings. When trade slackened, they fixed the control box on the lights to keep them red. But the ruse turned sour when a whole queue of traffic built up so that when the lights finally changed, 12 cars were wrecked and five people were hurt in the pile-up.

.　.　.

An effort in Turin to reduce traffic jams came to nothing when the bicycle loan scheme failed. On the first day only 8 of the 400 bikes were handed back.

.　.　.

Carmelo Silva, a paint salesman, was so annoyed

at being flagged down twice in an hour by the same policeman that he poured red paint all over him.

Unfortunately for Silva, the policeman was only stopping him to inform him that the earlier booking had been a mistake. Silva was fined £250 and ordered to paint the policeman's house.

. . .

In 1953, Dubliners were fiercely proud of their new £1 million bus station. The imposing seven-storey building of glass and marble, lofty columns and mosaic facings had taken seven years to complete.

The building offered 700 windows, 3,000 lights, 200 steps and 400 mahogany doors, but lacked one small thing. The officials had forgotten to install a clock so that the commuters using this outstanding building could actually catch their connections on time.

. . .

Tempers flared in Naples when a transport strike left commuters no means of getting home. In the riots that were sparked by the stoppage, almost the entire tram station at Porta Capuana was destroyed by fire. Rioters also set fire to four trolley buses, two trams and four buses. According to reporters, four injured bus conductors only narrowly escaped being lynched.

In 1962, an effigy of Mr Donald Gordon, president of Canadian Railways, was hanged and burned twice by French–Canadian demonstrators.

Their anger had been sparked over a comment made by Mr Gordon. He had asserted that the reason there were so few French-Canadians in senior railway jobs was the lack of suitably trained men. He also said that he would refuse to promote people simply because they were French-Canadian.

Agitators objecting to his statement called on the 'White Negroes of Quebec' to revolt 'like the patriots of 1837'.

.   .   .

In 1968 the people of Jakarta, Indonesia, saw their first red double-decker Leyland bus. Instantly named the Tall Red One by the locals, the bus then caused quite some fuss precisely because officials forgot that it *was* tall. Bridges in Jakarta had to be raised to allow the bus underneath, after a maiden voyage cockup when traffic on the principal highway stopped as the bus tried to squeeze under a pedestrian footbridge. 'We raised the road last week,' said one embarrassed city official at a welcoming ceremony.

Pedestrians cheered and clapped wherever the bus went, hoping that one day they too might get a ride on the Tall Red One. The bus, with a British capacity of 75, could hold 150 Indonesians, according to Jakarta officials.

A woman travelling from Sydney to Melbourne was driving down a narrow road with steep sides one dark evening when she entered a tunnel. Despite being a little perturbed because she didn't recall a tunnel on that particular route, she carried on.

After two miles of twisting and turning, she ran out of petrol. It was pitch dark, so she waited in her car for someone to turn up.

And turn up someone did. But not quite the kind of someone the lady was expecting. Her rescuer was not a passing motorist, but three miners. She had driven into a coal mine.

Yet even this lady had a commuting soulmate, albeit in distant Cincinnati, Ohio. Here it was that in fog, a woman drove carefully up a steep slope only to stall at the top. When she got out she discovered that she had driven onto a car transporter. Fortunately it was stationary.

. . .

A newly-married wife finally persuaded her husband to let her grandmother come and live with them. So the couple set off from their home in San Francisco to pick Granny up from Arizona. Driving their Volkswagen Beetle across the desert, they reached Granny's house, collected her and her luggage, and set off for home.

On their way back across the desert, Granny complained of being too hot. The couple pulled up and opened the back door so that she could sit on the floor of the car and cool her feet in the fresh air.

After a few minutes the girl asked Granny if she felt any cooler and on receiving no reply, discovered that, in fact, Granny had just expired from heat exhaustion.

Distressed and at a loss as to what to do in the middle of nowhere, the couple decided to drive on to the next gas station where they could make the necessary telephone calls. But a problem arose as what to do with Granny, because she was too big to lay down on the back seat.

Eventually, left with no option, the couple carefully wrapped her in a tarpaulin and lovingly tied her onto the roof-rack. When they reached the gas station, they left the car to make a few phone calls to the immediate family to inform them of the tragedy. When they came out of the phone booth they discovered that someone had stolen their car.

. . .

In South Carolina one hot day, Chuck Roberts, a farm labourer, was ploughing the fields. Overcome by thirst, Chuck decided the best way to keep cool would be to drink plenty of beer.

It was hot, and what with the alcohol, he became rather light-headed. Exactly how light-headed was demonstrated by the fact that when he finished work for the day and set off home on the motorway, he forgot to lift the cutting gear on the plough – with the result that he had torn up half a mile of road before the police flagged him down.

When the Washington Metro opened, it was plagued with problems. Automatic brakes locked, trains broke down in the morning and evening rush-hours, rain put some escalators out of order and some broke down of their own volition. Seven stations had to be shut when an under-river tunnel flooded, and then the automatic fare machines started spewing out free tickets.

But best of all (if you relish cockups), the aluminium carriages proved not to be strong enough to carry the extra load of commuters during peak times – small oversight, but these things happen. The added weight threw the automatic doors out of true and they refused to close. In order to right the situation, the carriages had to be emptied of all passengers. As one anguished and late passenger put it, 'They ought to scrap the whole thing, fill in the hole and give us our money back.'

. . .

A vital trainload of equipment was shunted right across the United States to a Ford plant. So important was the train's load that Ford insisted on being continually informed of its exact location. The moment it arrived at the plant, before it had been unloaded, an engine was coupled to the train by mistake. The engine proceeded to pull the vital consignment all the way back to its starting point.

. . .

One executive of the debt-ridden New York City Transit Authority put in an expense claim for £1,660. The claim was reimbursement for an 'inspection tour of the subway in Florence, Italy'.

Unfortunately, the executive did not get his expenses. For Florence, as one sharp-eyed accounts clerk – the kind of accounts clerk whose sharp eyes give you nightmares – observed, doesn't have a subway.

．　．　．

New York Subway passengers have become inventive at dodging fares. Teenagers have been seen to suck tokens back up through token slots, or squirt hairspray down the slots and then retrieve the tokens using thin strips of metal. Others take the path of least – or is it most? – resistance and simply jump the turnstiles. But if caught by the scores of undercover policemen who cruise the Subway, the offenders can expect to be punished by having to clean gum off the station floors.

On Manhattan buses, meanwhile, two fare dodgers made a notably bad move when they saw a bus idling at a kerb and mistook it for the regular service. It was in fact a roving police station used as a booking office for fare dodgers. The two climbed in the back doors hoping to avoid paying and walked straight into the arms of half a dozen plainclothes policemen.

．　．　．

An 11-year-old boy made a dream trip on the US railway by sleepwalking his way 100 miles to another town. In 1987, Michael Dixon was found walking barefoot along the tracks wearing just a T-shirt and pyjama pants. 'He hopped on a freight and wound up in Peru, Illinois,' said police chief Bill Page. 'He woke up, got off and thought he was still in his hometown of Danville.'

His mother said, 'He was having a nightmare. He sleepwalks but has never gone outside before.' Mrs Dixon said she had assumed that Michael was upstairs in bed until she got the phone call from the authorities in Peru.

. . .

A 50-year-old executive from Standard Oil of California hated flying so much that when he had to visit the company's Los Angeles branch for a week he took the train.

After the week was up, he took the overnight train back to San Francisco. On the train he met up with a rather attractive colleague and spent most of the journey in her compartment. When he awoke at Oakland he set off in his pyjamas to his own cabin, hoping no one would see him. To his horror, he discovered that during the night the section of the train which contained his compartment had been uncoupled and that his luggage and clothes were now heading northwards to Portland, Oregon. Remembering also that his wife had promised to meet him at the station did nothing for his rationality level, and he did the only thing he thought was left – clutched at his heart, groaned in great pain and called for an ambulance. When the train pulled in, he was immediately rushed to hospital where he enjoyed many visits and gifts from work colleagues and of course his wife, all deeply concerned at his 'heart' condition.

. . .

A Calcutta–Madras mail train reached the state of Andhra Pradesh with 800 tired passengers. It was nine days late.

. . .

British Transport Minister Roger Freeman managed a splendid gaffe (though, on the other hand, became briefly famous) when he suggested in 1992 that secretaries should use a new class of 'cheap and cheerful' train travel. Speculating about a multi-tiered commuter system, Mr Freeman suggested that the train would have a basic service for 'typists' and something 'more luxurious' for businessmen and civil servants. One transport watchdog commented sagely, 'I think he's put his foot in it.'

. . .

Radio 1 DJ Simon Bates, caught in a traffic snarl-up, was once forced to start his 9.30 a.m. Golden

Hour by car phone in the limousine taking him to Broadcasting House.

. . .

In 1942, Airey Neave and another prisoner escaped from Colditz disguised as Dutch electricians. Boarding a train full of early-morning workers, they found seats and one of them immediately fell asleep. He was woken by a sharp kick on the shins by his fellow escapee, because he had been speaking English in his sleep.

To circumvent problems the two changed trains, and to avoid becoming embroiled in a conversation with anyone they stood in the corridor rather than sat in a compartment.

After a while they were spotted by a large SS man who asked them if they were Jews. Establishing that they were not, the officer invited them to join him. After deflecting several suspicious questions and appearing to be as friendly as the tense situation allowed, the same man fell asleep again right beside the SS officer and snored happily for a couple of hours.

He was awoken by two military policemen tapping loudly on the glass door. They were inspecting documents. The SS man was so convinced of the men's false identities that he vouched for them. The two men later made it to Switzerland.

. . .

A young man and his girlfriend were lying in the long grass by the track at Stevenage, when the chap felt the need to relieve himself. Not wanting to leave his girlfriend for too long, he went to the bridge which crossed the train lines and started to urinate over it. There was a blinding flash as the urine hit the electrified lines and connected the gentleman to 25,000 volts. The young man was tossed into the air and spun down onto the track. Amazingly, he suffered only two broken bones – and, he said, a slight burning sensation.

. . .

British Rail's 1990 timetable was a classic. It contained over 1,000 errors and scheduled scores of ghost trains. A 76-page booklet, produced to correct the original errors, itself contained enough fresh mistakes for further correction to be necessary.

. . .

Queen Louise of Sweden was opening Stockholm's new underground system. With the dignity only a Queen can muster, she rode regally down the escalator, towards a banquet on the main platform of the Central station, where lunch was to be served on an eight-coach underground train. Then, as you would expect, a spectator spoiled everything by accidentally touching the emergency switch. The escalator juddered to a halt and went into reverse, leaving the Queen swaying and proceeding slightly less regally away from lunch. An engineer then stopped the escalator for a few seconds and started the Queen off downwards again.

. . .

New Zealand nursing sister Patricia Gregan went for a drink after work. She had six double Scotches at a hotel and missed her train home. The only option left at that time of night was a goods train, so Pat rode the 30 miles home perched astride the couplings between two trucks. Part of the ride went through a tunnel a mile and a half long. Pat was discovered straddling the trucks and was charged with travelling on a portion of a goods train not intended for passengers, and with being on railway property while being intoxicated – well, just a bit.

. . .

The dawn traffic in Madrid one September morning was noticeably quieter than usual. The normal chaos had been reduced because 50 trams were trapped in their depot. Council workers had resurfaced the road outside during the night. Somehow, they had failed to notice the tramlines.

. . .

1989 was election time in Japan, and a politician from the opposition Socialist Party was on his way to address a public meeting. He realized to his horror that he was on the wrong train – the train he was on was scheduled to go straight to Tokyo without stopping at the station he needed. After a heated argument, he finally persuaded the guard to make an unscheduled stop so that he could jump off in time for his meeting. The next morning, of course, the politician was obliged to resign – the papers had publicized the fact that as a result of his action the train had arrived in Tokyo a whole two minutes late.

. . .

A gentleman on his way home on British Rail was threatened by a drunkard with a knife. The maniac lunged at him just as the train pulled into a station, so the man leapt nimbly out of the carriage and ran down the platform to the guard's van. Once inside, he explained to the guard what had just happened. The guard blanched, and with commendable concern for the other passengers locked both himself and proposed victim into his van.

. . .

Ernie Beha was named the greatest railway sleeper of them all. The Southern Region champion, Ernie earned his title by sleeping through Dorking North, Effingham Junction, Chislehurst, Margate and Folkestone. He has also slept through his home station of Ewell West more times than he and his wife care to remember.

'The trouble began back in 1935,' he explained ruefully. 'I moved from Tufnell Park in London to Ewell in Surrey. On my first journey home I dozed off and woke up at Effingham Junction, 16 miles down the line. Travelling seems to affect me in a curious way. I just can't keep awake in a train. It's the rhythm of the wheels.'

To combat his problem, Ernie has primed the porters at Ewell West to keep an eye out for him. This system doesn't always succeed as the porters are often very busy, and 18-stone Ernie in mid-snooze can be an intimidating sight for a commuter who isn't aware of his compulsion for forty winks.

On one occasion Ernie did not see his wife and family for three nights. For three nights he slept through Ewell West station. For three mornings he repeated the performance, going the other way after spending the night at three different hotels. 'On the fourth night,' said Ernie, 'I was desperate. I left Waterloo station with a peace offering of two dozen carnations for the wife. When I got in at 1 a.m. I had one left.' What happened was that Ernie had dozed off all the way to Leatherhead and had paid a man to take him back by motorbike. 'For some reason,' recalled Ernie, 'I didn't get the hang of pillion-riding and 23 carnations disappeared into the night.'

. . .

Antony Weaver, director of the Clerkenwell Heritage Centre, was on the way to take his aged parents to see *The Phantom Of The Opera* after waiting several months for the tickets. Having to change trains at Nuneaton, he went to collect his bicycle from the guard's van as the train approached the station. The conductor asked him to return to his seat. Mr Weaver explained his mission and tried to walk past, whereupon the collector arrested him for alleged assault, and when the train pulled into the station he called the transport police. An incredulous Mr Weaver was taken swiftly to Nuneaton Police Station where he was locked in a cell for three hours with no opportunity to give his side of the story.

As his parents waited anxiously at King's Cross, Mr Weaver was charged with various offences. Seeing *The Phantom Of The Opera* stood not a ghost of a chance. Some time later all charges were dropped and Mr Weaver's arrest was declared unlawful.

. . .

A homing pigeon – well, it is a sort of commuter – released in Pembrokeshire one day failed to reappear that evening. Eleven years later, not so much exhausted as deeply dead, the bird turned up in a box postmarked Brazil. 'We had given it up for lost,' commented the owner.

2

A Funny Thing Happened on the Way

A MR FLEMING from Fulham wrote to the *Evening Standard* in 1992 to describe a scene on a Heathrow-bound Piccadilly Line train. Facing three foreign travellers, he observed them counting the number of stations on the chart above.

When the train pulled into Terminal Four, they sat and listened intently to the announcement which said: 'This is Terminal Four, all passengers for this terminal must alight here.'

The three exchanged bemused glances, one pointed to where the announcement had come from, while another pointed at the 'no smoking' sign plastered on the window.

When the message was repeated for the second time, the three shrugged their shoulders, pulled out their cigarettes, carefully lit them and puffed them dutifully until the train reached the next terminal.

Mr Fleming's experience proved what we were beginning to suspect – that if you commute long enough, eventually you will find something to laugh about . . . .

· · ·

Chris Tarrant described on London's Capital Radio the sad case of a Milan commuter who skidded on his moped, crashed into a tree and broke both legs. A passing motorist called an ambulance. It rushed to the scene, skidded and crashed into another tree. As it crunched to a halt, its back door flew open and hit the moped rider on the head, fracturing his skull. The commuter was later said by the hospital to be 'comfortable'.

. . .

Miss Sarah Ainsworth from Herts recalled a journey she made on the Bakerloo Line one evening. She noticed an ordinary grey-suited, grey-faced commuter who was so unremarkable that she took no more notice of him. That was, however, until he stood up to leave. Placing his briefcase carefully on the floor, he stretched up, grabbed hold of two hand straps, threw himself back and performed a perfect somersault. Then without a word, he straightened his suit, picked up his briefcase and left the train.

. . .

Sir Denis Thatcher once found himself on a BR train, where he was joined in his compartment by an outing of patients from an institution. Their minder began a head count, and reached five before he got to Sir Denis. 'Who are you?' asked the puzzled minder. 'The Prime Minister's husband, actually,' he replied. 'Oh, of course. Six, seven, eight . . . .'

. . .

John Drew of Billericay, Essex, was on a domestic flight in Venezuela when the captain started speaking excitedly in Spanish. 'Half the passengers ran forwards screaming,' he related. 'I adopted the crash position. Then a stewardess asked me if I would like to pass my camera to the pilot as we were approaching Angel Falls.'

. . .

The 17.42 from Romiley, Greater Manchester, to New Mills, Derbyshire, might have been renamed the Glorious 12.10 when it was delayed because the driver, surrounded by three other BR staff, was plucking a pheasant on the platform. 'I think it's disgusting. He's paid to drive trains, not pluck pheasants,' commuter Liz Shaw enunciated carefully.

. . .

Cecil Parkinson, then Transport Secretary, was on his way to open a new station in Hampshire in May 1990 when his train broke down.

. . .

In January 1988, Lord Snowdon attacked British Rail for locking him inside a metal cage with a flock of squawking chickens on a trip from Brighton to London. During the journey, on which he was accompanying a wheelchair-bound friend, the

Queen's former brother-in-law shouted for 30 minutes to be set free before a guard heard him.

. . .

The *Daily Mail* journalist Vincent Mulchrone was stuck between stations thirsty and out of cigarettes. Just at that moment, a Waterloo–Portsmouth express also got stuck with its buffet car alongside Mulchrone's carriage. Exploiting the coincidence, he opened the window, stretched across the gap and beat on the windows until finally they opened and a face appeared. 'Would you get me some cigarettes?' begged Vince. The Face complied and then asked, 'Will you have a drink?' Making the most of the offer, Vince had four miniatures – the equivalent of ten small Scotches. Then his only problem was how to explain to his wife how he got in such a state on a train she knew not to have a buffet.

. . .

In 1987, commuters at Notting Hill Gate Tube Station watched as two blind men kept on bumping into one another. They backed off, tried again and once more clashed white sticks. 'Some maniac keeps bumping into me,' cried one of the men.

Eventually the ticket collector stepped in to separate them. 'Hold on,' he told them, 'just hold on. You're both blind.'

'Good God,' exclaimed the other blind man. 'I thought I was prepared for anything.'

. . .

Doreen Allinson sets off for work in the morning by boat. She crosses the half mile of Ullswater from her home at Blowick House to work in a tourist information caravan at Glenridding, and only the roughest weather will prevent her from making the trip six days a week, six months of the year.

Once, however, she took her four children, to drop them off for school. That day it was foggy, and she dropped them off on what she believed to be the other side. It was in fact on an island about 25 yards from the shore. Luckily, she realized just as she set off back home and could rescue them.

. . .

A granny ceated havoc in August 1986 by cycling down to the shops – along the fast lane of the M25. Stunned motorists raised the alarm when they passed the septuagenarian pedalling merrily along four miles of motorway towards Egham in Surrey.

It took an RAC patrolman to steer her to the safety of the hard shoulder, where a policeman popped her and her bike into his car and took her home to Chertsey. The policeman said generously: 'We will not report her.'

. . .

When Sean Edmeads, a bird fancier, broke down on the M25 he decided not to phone for help. Instead he set off two racing pigeons to his home near Sevenoaks in Kent, with a message for his father. Mr Edmeads Snr, alerted by the airmail message, arrived on the scene at the same time as traffic police.

. . .

A businessman was caught running across all three lanes of the M25, dodging cars as he tried to catch invoices which had escaped from a case on his roof-rack. A Czech lorry driver was spotted on the same road taking photographs of his vehicle on the hard shoulder. Another driver was caught driving without a seat belt, while talking on a portable phone and reading a map. He was so angry at being stopped that he lodged an official complaint with the Chief Constable of Hertfordshire.

. . .

The Irish national transport system had a surprise when £776,000 worth of new diesel locomotives arrived from America. When the driver got in to test the first engine, he discovered as he coasted out of the station that he could not see the track. The solution was simple if embarrassing. It was decided to drive the trains backwards. A railway official explained: 'When run this way round the driver's view is obstructed. On the main lines we are now running them the wrong way round. It doesn't affect the speed.'

(Foot-plate footnote: one of the first locomotives on a back-to-front run crashed.)

. . .

The usual instruction period for train drivers in Nigeria was cut in 1968 from five years to eighteen months, on account of the civil war. The railway bosses called the quick instruction spell a 'crash course'.

However, they were still smarting from the Biafra Radio taunts which came thick and fast after their previous 'crash course'. Two engines had set off at different times from different towns on the same line. They crashed head-on.

. . .

Problems began in the West Midlands town of Stourbridge when the bus garage closed to save money and 40 out of 112 drivers left.

Crews from depots in other areas came to replace them and had to learn the town's 30 routes quickly. To help them along, regular passengers sat on the bus and shouted out the directions. 'We are grateful to passengers for helping the drivers out,' a Passenger Transport Executive said. 'There have only been a small number of mistakes.'

. . .

Rocco Carosiello, an Italian-born bus driver from London Transport, took great pride in his job. So when a mechanical inspector – on board to check his driving – gave him the verdict 'You have given me a fairly good ride', it was like a red rag to a bull.

Mr Carosiello told the mechanical inspector that if he could do any better, he should drive the bus himself. With that he jumped out of the cab and, leaving his 50 passengers marooned, caught a bus home.

Later Mr Carosiello said he was sorry for the passengers, but it was a matter of principle. Defending his driving, Mr Carosiello said: 'I am a jolly good driver and it upset me when this bloke said I was driving fairly well. It was the way he said it. I took it that he was hinting that my driving was not up to standard.'

. . .

Jo Stevenson from Finsbury Park tells of the time she caught her usual number 19 bus from Finsbury Park.

When the bus stopped at Green Park a woman got off and had a quick word with the driver who turned and looked down the bus with a puzzled expression. At that moment a black cab pulled up in front of the bus and the conductor jumped out. He explained that he had nipped off the bus in Highbury to buy a paper. While he was in the shop, someone on the bus had rung the bell and off it had gone – leaving the conductor behind. He was left no option but to hop in a taxi and shout 'Follow that bus'.

. . .

Passengers on the number 5 bus route in Warwickshire had to get off and walk every time the bus crossed the 92-year-old bridge at Luddington.

As the bus approached the bridge, the conductor had to count the passengers. Thirty-five lucky passengers were allowed to stay on the bus, while the rest had to disembark and hot-foot it across the bridge to catch the bus on the other side.

Railway surveyors had imposed a ten-and-a-half ton weight limit on the bridge, and double-decker buses capable of carrying 75 people reach that limit when 35 are on board. Additional passengers had to walk.

An official of the Stratford Blue company said there were no hard-and-fast rules about who was ordered off and who wasn't: 'It's left to the discretion and good sense of the conductor.' He added cautiously, 'There have been no complaints yet.'

. . .

New Yorkers couldn't believe their eyes when dozens of decorators set about repainting their grimy, graffiti-covered Subway stations.

Unfortunately their disbelief was well-founded, for after a couple of days the painters downed tools and disappeared, complaining that they had not been paid.

Police then arrested 63-year-old Vincent Pannone and accused him of defrauding the painters of at least £12,000. It transpired that Pannone had not been contracted to do the work by anyone. Acting on his own, he had attracted the painters by handing out leaflets at supermarkets and promising them £55 a day providing that they put up some £600 each for 'insurance' purposes. The £600, he assured them, would be repaid at a later date.

The trick left Mr Pannone with a lot of explaining to do to the police, and the city's transport authority with the small problem of 700 platform pillars painted in black and white up to only six feet and several dozen half-painted tunnels and bridges.

. . .

A woman who thought she was doing her duty by prodding her umbrella into the snoring form of a passenger on the 6.05 a.m. from Luton to St Pancras was mortally embarrassed when she found that the man was fully awake and the snoring was coming from the dog at his feet.

. . .

Anne O'Neill became a Cinderella on the rails and met a Prince Charming in the shape of British Rail guard Tony Marshall. Anne was boarding the 7.23

a.m. at Greater Manchester when she lost her shoe between the platform and the track. Having visions of hobbling through city streets in just one high heel, she looked round for someone to help her. Along came Tony, who told her not to worry. Tony sprinted up to the driver and asked him to reverse the engine. Passengers on board began to worry when the train started going backwards instead of forwards. Tony then scrambled onto the line, rescued the shoe and presented it to Anne while the passengers applauded. 'It was nothing really,' Tony said. 'The damsel was in distress and we are pleased to be of service.'

. . .

Transport strikes in cities have the knack of bringing out unsuspected reserves of ingenuity in commuters. Sharon Beattie, aged 19, got to work despite a rail strike in 1989. Zooming through Aldwych on roller skates borrowed from her younger brother, she yelled to a TV crew, 'I'll never shout at him again, I've never been this early for work.'

. . .

Passengers on the Cambridge to London line were approached by two young men in white coats. They announced that they were from the Ministry of Agriculture and were investigating an outbreak of foot and mouth disease on a farm near Cambridge. They explained patiently that the disease was thought to be carried south on the shoes of passengers. The two men then asked the passengers to take off their shoes and hand them over so that the soles could be tested for traces of infection.

Every single passenger complied quietly and no one was in the least suspicious until the train pulled into King's Cross and they had still not had their shoes returned. More to the point, the two young men in the white coats were nowhere to be seen. Out on the platform, however, were several hundred pairs of shoes all tied together in odd pairs. The young men were not in fact from any Ministry at all – they were students on a rag-week stunt.

. . .

In 1985, Linda Taylor was sitting on the Tyneside Metro when the driver announced that he had a postcard for her. The card had been sent by a fellow commuter. It was addressed to Linda and the Gang, the 7.24 West Monkseaton to Walkergate Metro, via the driver, Monday to Friday only, Newcastle, England. The postman was at the station early to ensure that Linda received her special delivery.

The driver came on the tannoy to inform passengers that he had a postcard for someone on this train called Linda. Linda said: 'It was sent by a man called Ken whom I only know from catching the train in the morning.' Linda sent her congratulations to the Post Office for tracking her down.

A spokesman for the Post Office said, 'It is unlikely that we'd send a postman running after the train. The card was probably delivered to the driver. We're rather proud of our detective work.'

. . .

Philip White of the 125 Commuters Club recalls the time when his train stopped with only one carriage next to the platform. The voice which came over the speakers lamented: 'British Rail regrets we are a total failure.'

. . .

Conceivably the ultimate, nightmare commuting experience fell to Spike Milligan's publisher, Jack Hobbs, when he suffered the embarrassing result of eating something which did not agree with him. Hobbs rushed squelching into an Oxford Street store and demanded a new pair of trousers, which, to his impatience, the assistant spent ages parcelling up. Rushing out, parcel under his arm, Hobbs raced to Waterloo just in time to catch his train. Once on board he headed straight for the lavatory where, removing his own trousers with relief, he joyously threw them out of the window. He then unwrapped his parcel to find in it the beautiful fluffy pink cardigan that the assistant had so lovingly wrapped for him.

. . .

Another commuter visited the lavatory on a train, taking his automatic umbrella with him. Once he was inside, the mechanism on the umbrella somehow activated and the umbrella shot open. Unable to shut it, the gentleman was forced to stay put until rescued by BR staff.

. . .

British Rail reportedly scored an own goal when Professor Rowland Smith, Manchester United chairman, complained about fleas on an Edinburgh sleeper. His 'personal' letter of apology from Sir Bob Reid, BR's Chairman, had a memo inadvertently left on it saying: 'Send standard flea letter.'

. . .

Mrs Maureen Allason was left with conflicting information when a driver at Tonbridge contradicted the guard's timetable advice. 'That little chap?' he said. 'He don't know nothing – he's only been here 10 years.' A driver at the same station announced to commuters over the tannoy, 'This train is due to arrive in Tunbridge Wells, er, sometime later today.'

. . .

At a golf course in Petersfield, Hampshire, stayaway commuters using a strike as an excuse to practise their putting were a bit miffed to find themselves held up behind a party of 26 British Rail workers.

.   .   .

A young man from Tottenham was saying his goodbyes to his girlfriend Patricia at Upminster Tube Station. The service being as it is these days, they had plenty of time to kiss and talk before the train arrived. When it eventually drew into the station, the lovers locked into a passionate clinch. As Patricia got on board, a voice on the tannoy announced: 'Nice going, young love is so beautiful.' Continuing in more professional tones, the announcer informed passengers that 'due to circumstances beyond our control' the westbound train would be delayed for a further five minutes. Exploiting the opportunity afforded to them by BR's punctuality, the young lovers used the extra time to kiss for a final time. As the sliding door started to shut, the voice came over the tannoy again, not with an announcement but with a tuneful rendition of 'Strangers in the night, across the platform, da, da, da, da, da . . . .'

.   .   .

Lord Lichfield had an aged relative who preferred to travel in less crowded compartments. For train journeys this gentleman would swap his impeccable pinstripe and bowler for a tattered cloth-cap and old raincoat. Instead of carrying a newspaper, he always took an orange.

Once he had found himself a seat, he would whip this orange out of his pocket and start to peel it at great speed. This frenzy used to attract the attention of all those around him, and once he had their full attention he would hold the orange-peel in one hand and then throw the orange out of the window.

The curiosity of the other commuters would overcome their stiff upper lips and one of them would ask him what he was doing. The gentleman would stare at the questioning individual and retort, 'I don't like oranges.' As a result, the gentleman had as much space as he desired.

3

Ethics Man

COMMUTING IS A strange, artificial activity – it is hard to imagine monkeys and dogs submitting to its disciplines, though sheep and lemmings, possibly. The successful mass transportation of commuters relies above all on the good manners of travellers, their drivers and conductors. Just one breach of the unwritten rules of the game can cause mayhem. Talking loudly, reading other people's newspapers, eating, staring (indeed focusing on any point other than a vague middle distance) and farting are among the taboos, but there are many, many others. Here, we look at the ethics of (probably) mankind's most peculiar activity, starting with a delve into Miss Manners' Guide To Excruciatingly Correct Behaviour, in which the ethical guru-ette is asked a question we have all agonized upon . . .

Dear Miss Manners,

My question is on subway etiquette. I often meet a co-worker whom I do not like on the subway; we are heading for the same destination. May I say hello and go further down the platform in order to read my book? Saying, on a sunny day, that I must run back to the office for my umbrella is losing its credibility.

Gentle Reader,

The instrument you require is in your hands and it is not an umbrella. All travellers should carry books, whether they read or not, as weapons of defence against conversational assault. You need not move along the platform after you have greeted your colleague politely; merely move your nose downward towards your open book. If the person says anything more than a return hello, you pause, look up with a puzzled smile, and say slowly, 'What?' as if awakening from a deep sleep. If the statement is repeated, you reply 'Oh,' with another vague smile, and then return to the book. Two or three rounds of whats and ohs should polish off even a determined talker.

. . .

The Guinness Book of Records lists the first bus service in the world as being inaugurated on 12 April 1903 between Eastbourne railway station and Meads in East Sussex. Within days of this momentous event, the world's first complaint about the buses was printed in an anonymous letter to the *Eastbourne Chronicle*.

'DOES THE BUS TRAVEL TOO FAST?' yelled the headline above the letter. 'The new motor omnibus should not be allowed to go so fast down Meads Hill,' the writer demanded. 'When I rode it today it seemed to take a sudden plunge down the decline and rushed past the next road at what I should say was quite 20 miles an hour.' The complaint went on to list near misses with a horse and cart and a water cart, and concluded, 'If private motorists choose to risk their necks, the driver of a public motor car is hardly justified in endangering the lives of passengers.'

. . .

In 1978, China set a new example by appealing for comradely criticism of its railway workers. On the Peking–Shanghai express the passengers were asked to note whether the carriages were kept clean and whether the refreshment service was good. The best workers would get a red banner which they would have to hand over to anyone on the next trip who did any better. Passenger delegates met railway workers in the dining car to decide who would receive the award. The designated attendant was then presented with a banner and applauded for his 'good deeds, warmth and thoughtfulness'.

In 1990, on British Rail, on the other hand, a competition was launched to 'name your friendly railwayman'. The award, offered by the Transport Users' Consultative Committee for Southern England, was for railway workers who had performed acts of kindness and courtesy but whose efforts had gone unsung. Passengers obviously refused to sing, for out of 20,000 possible ticket collectors, porters or buffet-car attendants to be nominated, a grand total of 10 recommendations were received.

. . .

In 1990, rush-hour drivers came across two cars in a head-on smash. The impatient drivers got out of their cars, moved the damaged vehicles to one side, ignored the passengers trapped inside and sped off home. The police condemned the drivers as 'heartless' for abandoning 76-year-old George Martin and his wife, 81-year-old Dorothy.

. . .

A juggernaut and a bulldozer met in a narrow road in Bonn. Both drivers refused to budge. For a while the two sat glaring at one another. Then tempers gave way. First the lorry rammed the bulldozer, then the bulldozer shattered the truck's windscreen with its mechanical shovel. The fight continued with more and more wreckage wrought and still neither driver giving way. After £7,000 worth of damage, the drivers gave up and were fined £400 each.

. . .

A female British journalist visited France in 1987 to experience the sort of driving that had resulted in 118 deaths and 1,528 injuries in one weekend. As she drove out of a car-park exit, the monsieur behind berated her for moving too slowly through the exit barrier by repeatedly sounding his horn. In response, the young lady grimaced at him in her rear-view mirror. Once out on the open road, he pulled alongside and proceeded to scold her for her lack of *politesse*.

. . .

The style of French drivers reflects the way they live, claimed the head of an accident unit in Birmingham. The British are territorial and so gave other cars a wide berth, but the French live huddled in apartment blocks and drive the same way. Apparently, it's common in all Latin countries, where people live close together, for drivers to snuggle up to one another – to the cosy extent that on a road like the Paris Périphérique or any German autobahn, you can see the whites of the driver's eyes behind you.

. . .

Thirty bus mechanics in Sydney staged a demonstration when the Leyland buses they looked after were replaced by 500 Mercedes vehicles. Far from showing solidarity with the mother country, the mechanics were angry that the German buses were so reliable compared with the British that their jobs were at risk. As a final and ironical insult, it emerged during the mêlée following this news that the Mercedes buses were being shipped from Germany in bits to be assembled down under – at Leyland's Australian plant.

. . .

Vienna electrician Karl Emminger had been to a party. Soon after midnight, he was waiting at a bus stop in the cold and rain when a bus driven by Oskar Schillab drove past without stopping. Karl hailed a taxi and ordered it to 'follow that bus'. At the first traffic lights, Karl, 38, got out of the cab and punched Oskar, 39, on the nose. Dazed, Oskar let his foot off the brake, and the bus chugged merrily into a dress-shop window. At his trial, Karl was ordered to pay £1,667 damages. But he became a national hero in Austria, receiving fan letters from all over the country.

. . .

In 1944 Earl Poulett and his young wife were ordered out of their railway carriage by a British officer with a sten gun. The officer wanted the carriage for two German prisoners of war, and Earl and Lady Poulett had to stand in a bitterly cold corridor for 5 hours. When the Earl complained in the House of Lords, it transpired that theirs was not the only story of hardship; there were occasions when trains packed with standing civilians pulled up alongside others loaded with grinning Germans, each with a seat to themselves.

Another incident involved 14 civilians standing

in a freezing corridor while five captured German officers smoked and ate chocolate in a heated compartment. When a complaint was made to the railway inspector he claimed he was powerless in the matter, but would make sure that the blinds were closed so that the passengers would not have the 'extra humiliation of watching'.

. . .

Ron Wilson took out his frustration about an impending rail strike on a BR railwayman and then was forced to apologize. Ron, a 50-year-old accountant, got so het up over the thought of the money he would lose in business and hotel bills due to the strike that when he got off the train he lambasted the first porter he came across.

Soon, the strike was called off and the next day Ron was able to catch his usual train to work. But as the train drew into Charing Cross he was joined in the buffet by a uniformed BR official who told him to get off the train and apologize to the porter he had shouted at. Ron said, 'There was the man I had confronted, with another BR man and a policeman. The policeman said nothing – he just stood there, but he was evidently there for a reason. It felt like Big Brother catching up with me. I said I was sorry. I was very rough on the man, but I didn't expect this sort of humiliation.

Another commuter who saw the whole affair said: 'Ron did what most of us feel like doing so often when there is a strike. He sounded off, there is no doubt. But this apology that he was forced to make was amazing.' So what did the famous BR spokesman have to say about the whole thing? 'If a member of staff has been abused or slandered by a passenger, he is just as entitled to an apology as anyone else.'

. . .

Regular commuters on the District Line witness the performance of a young man dressed for the building site. He sidles up to the nearest unsuspecting fellow passenger with the friendly invitation: 'My friends and I meet every Tuesday to study the Bible, would you like to join us?' As a layman drumming up support, he fails every time, but as a Machiavelli trying to get a bit more elbow room, he is incredibly successful.

. . .

In the first half of the nineteenth century, passengers refused to pay the rising fares for first-class carriages and opted instead to travel in the second- or third-class compartments, which were substantially cheaper.

This boycott was initiated by Lord Worsley, who won the support of the press but not, as you can imagine, the railways. So when an association of wealthy passengers was formed, who wore badges proudly proclaiming that they were third-class travellers, the railways decided to take action.

The Manchester and Leeds Railway introduced the Soot-Bag System and the Farmyard Foul-Up. Some hours before the train was due to leave, small bands of chimney sweeps were ushered into the third-class carriages set aside for distinguished travellers like Lord Worsley and told to empty the contents of their bags over the floors. Then pigs and sheep were locked in the carriage long enough for their more compelling odours to permeate the train.

Such methods have long since been abandoned, or so it is claimed.

. . .

Passengers using the Long Island Railroad used to be able to get a chit signed by the station master verifying that their train was late in arriving at Penn Central station in New York. In the morning secretaries grabbed them for their bosses, in the evening the bosses grabbed them – for their wives. Those chits were quite common. In Japan, little certificates confirming that a commuter train was late, and that the blame lies entirely with the railway, are the norm – but very rare indeed, since the trains are hardly ever late. All the folklore about the punctuality of Japanese commuter trains is correct. Foreigners can find their way about on the railways even with such optimistic instructions as 'You'll know you're at the right station when you've been travelling for 32 minutes and 30 seconds.'

A US minister and his family were forced to sit up all night when the Amtrak sleeping car they had already paid for was not added to the train. When the minister tried to complain, the attendant told him: 'Listen Mac, I don't want to hear about your problems. I've had a lousy trip myself . . . .'

．　．　．

Dermot Lewis of St Albans, Hertfordshire, was worried about the loneliness of the long-distance commuter and so suggested that people who wanted to chat on the train should wear a blue-topped pin in their buttonhole. Not surprisingly, that plan didn't come to much. But there has been serious research on the ways commuters try to keep themselves to themselves. In 1979, experiments were carried out to examine what happens when people's 'personal space' is invaded. The offended person will frown, blush or take avoiding action. If close contact is forced upon them, say on an overcrowded train, they subconsciously turn the intruders into non-persons and look straight through them.

The survey also revealed that Germans require the largest area of personal space, then come the English, Americans and Latin Americans. The French require even less space, with the Arabs topping the list as those ready to exist at particularly close quarters.

The Japanese, of course, are famous for their sphinx-like tolerance of packed commuter trains –

those pushers employed to encourage commuters to move-along-inside-the-car-please really exist. It is estimated that about 80 of these 'pushers' are required for each train. Extra pushers are recruited in winter when more muscle power is needed to get passengers into the trains, because of the excess space taken up by winter clothing.

. . .

Some cultures may positively like being sardined together, but the Japanese don't pretend to have any affection for their commuting hell. They actually have the world's worst commuting manners.

No Japanese, for example, would be surprised by the experience of Catherine Mack of Wood Green, who was killing time on her train journey home by reading a book. Simultaneously she turned a page and crossed her legs, accidentally tapping the shin of a businessman standing next to her. Apologizing and assuring him that it was an accident did no good; the businessman snapped, 'Well, I don't see why you have to cross your legs in the rush hour.'

Japanese Railways are at least keen to upgrade the manners of their staff, if not their passengers, whose only real concession to civilized behaviour is not all to breathe in at the same time. In 1988, 12,000 Japanese rail employees were taught *politesse* – including how to smile with their eyes. At two-day classes, station staff and guards were taken through their paces by former Japan Airline stewardesses: 'Hand over mouth,' they were told. 'Practise smiling with your eyes. Show no teeth.' The charm training – named MASK (Manners, Attitude, Smile, Kindness) – seems to have paid off. When staff lend passengers money, it comes from their own pockets and is not reimbursed.

. . .

British Rail executive Andrew Goodman tells of the unwritten rule of non-communication that prevades some early-morning journeys. On one occasion a wasp was flying round his compartment. Finally it came to rest on one gentleman's lap, crawled up his newspaper and onto his shirt. The rest of the carriage watched mesmerized, but not one of them thought of warning the gentleman whose shirt they were all watching so avidly.

Some lines are the exception to the rule, however. The Brighton Line is famous for its sociability – at least three trains hold their own Christmas parties, complete with decorations and paper hats. Through their Commuter Associations, City workers play 'Paintball' survivalist games at the weekend. Once, they even played against a team of BR workers.

. . .

There was once a tradition that on their last home journey retiring London commuters would spin their bowler hat off the train and into the Thames. An alternative was de-rimming the redundant bowler. Thus did Bill Coleman, a City accountant, end 24 years of commuting on the Witham–Liverpool Street service. Clutching his de-rimmed bowler with a champagne cork stuck in it, Mr Coleman said surprisingly, 'We've had some happy times, but now I'm retiring the train journey is all I'm going to miss.'

. . .

In the 1860s accidents were so frequent that the London, Chatham and Dover railway was renamed the London, Smashem and Turnover. Cashing in on this problem in an attempt to boost circulation figures, one national magazine sank to the depths of offering £100 in free insurance to the next-of-kin of any passenger killed in a rail accident. That was providing, of course, that the victim had a copy of the magazine in his pocket at the time.

. . .

In 1959, the railways in Britain had become so bad that the churches were praying for them, Lord Lucas revealed in the House of Lords. He also disclosed that one church in Oxford had forfeited prayer for action and that petitions had been organized from the pulpit. In one church 600 commuting Christians signed.

In 1962, the actress Katie Boyle reportedly kept a train waiting while she walked her Pekinese dogs. Miss Boyle was concerned that her two Pekes, Olitzi and Tai-Tai, were not quite ready for the 170-mile journey from Exeter to London. 'What can I do?' she asked a worried porter. 'The dogs can't travel all that way without a walk first.' As the Pekes scampered on a grass verge, the porter pleaded with them to hurry up. It was only when the guard waved his flag that Ms Boyle picked up the dogs and ran to her compartment.

. . .

The chicest present from a Swedish husband to his wife used to be a 50-krona (£4) transport card. This monthly pass allowed unlimited travel on all public transport in the Greater Stockholm area. Sweden is also believed to have one of the highest suicide rates in the world. There might be a link between these two facts.

. . .

Norwegian Railways have a commitment to being kind to their customers. In January 1989, an Oslo woman was anxious at the thought of a seven-hour train journey without being able to smoke. So she visited the state railway system to complain about the lack of smoking compartments.

The result was that when she set off on her long journey, she had a carriage all to herself. She said,

'I'd rather sit on my own and have the chance to puff than sit around and mope with all the non-smokers.'

A railway spokesman explained: 'It'll cost us a bit more to fix up a smoking carriage. But it's good to be nice, even if Christmas has gone.'

. . .

In 1966, nine volunteers donned special headgear in order to allow the study of head movements during rail motion. The study was being conducted by Dr Walsh of Edinburgh University, whose own young daughter acted as one of the guinea pigs. The hats were fitted with special lamps and mirrors for the occasion. The result of the professor's study indicated a sideways tilting of the head during rail travel that is only usually observed in states of severe inebriation. Dr Walsh concluded that a train journey could be quite uncomfortable. BR said his conclusions had been noted.

But should a railway company perform such experiments on passengers without their knowledge? Travellers on the New York Subway were surreptitiously subjected to tests using a 'harmless' bacteriological agent by the United States Army. The exercise, carried out in June 1966, was designed to assess the vulnerability of American subway systems to bacteriological warfare.

The agent chosen, *Bacillus subtili yar niger*, was darkened with charcoal and then sprinkled on the floor of the station. In addition, small quantities of the germ were sprayed through the gratings in the street above to be sucked into the station.

At one point, an aerosol cloud of the agent covered a train while it was in the station, but when the cloud engulfed passengers getting off the train, they brushed their clothing, looked at the grating and then simply walked away.

. . .

Researchers eventually turned their attentions to problems Japanese. After months of grappling with the problem of commuter stress (and apparently much else), Japan's Railway Labour Science Research Institute concluded that the seven million male passengers who sardine into Tokyo each day should cuddle up to the nearest pretty girl. Some commuters had long taken this advice without the help of scientists. Japanese women list the worst wandering-hands-offenders as executives, civil servants and journalists.

However, a group of five English teachers in Tokyo decided that even if Japanese women would not complain, they should air their own grievances. In a letter to the *Japan Times*, the five gave this explicit warning: 'Japanese businessmen beware. We have passively endured your abuse on the crowded trains and subways for six months. You have finally pushed us past our point of tolerance and non-reprisal. . . . Why must your sneaky, loathsome, roaming hands take advantage of our vulnerability in packed trains? If you don't stop debasing us, we shall reciprocate by crushing your insteps, elbowing you and shouting . . . .'

This letter received wide publicity in Japan and women were advised to stick needles into offenders' thighs or shout loudly at them. But it appeared that the gropers were developing thick skins, for when one woman screamed at her molester, he shouted back 'If you don't like it, why the hell don't you take a taxi to work instead of a crowded train?'

. . .

Robertson Cumming, a bus driver in Durban, came to the end of his tether. So angered was he by complaints and interference from his passengers that he got out of his cab and left them in the middle of a busy road.

This was not before he had shouted: 'Get someone else to drive your bus, I have had enough,' or words to that effect.

Cumming then made his way to headquarters, where he handed in his resignation.

Cumming had finally snapped because after an endless stream of criticism from passengers, one had pointed out that he was driving down the wrong street.

. . .

In 1990, Barry 'Brakeshoe' Schwartz was left no

option but to take a $15 cab ride to a meeting of the Hobo Club in a Beverly Hills bar. The bus driver had refused to take him because he looked too scruffy.

Ironically enough, 'Brakeshoe' Schwartz is not a real down and out, but a pretend one, and this rejection represented a considerable personal achievement. During the week he pursues his career as a video-maker, but at the weekend he indulges his hobby of being a vagabond. Donning wayfarer gear, he spends his two free days jumping freight trains and generally just hanging out.

America's new part-time leisure-hobos have jobs, homes, credit cards and cars, and pay £10 to sign up as a member of the National Hobo Association. About 4,000 members attend regular meetings and receive a newsletter full of on-the-rail advice.

Sheri 'Hometown' Doyle completed her thesis at the University of California while on train-hopping wanderlusters. She claims that hobo culture is a serious anthropological phenomenon and that those who are attracted to weekends in the freightcar become part of a distinguished American tradition.

The railways, however, see the phenomenon in a rather different light. According to spokeswoman Cathy Westphal, 'Yuppie hobos set a bad example. I can't tell you how many kids get their legs cut off while trying to hop moving trains.'

Indeed, members of the National Hobo Association refer to train wheels as 'salami slicers', but that is all part of the gypsy glamour. 'In the old days it was need and desperation,' said actor Garth Bishop, editor of *Hobo News*. 'Now it's a weekend vacation adventure.'

.   .   .

In Dallas, Texas, the transport authority painted its fleet of single-decker buses bright pink, adorned the fronts with a nose and two buck teeth and stuck three-foot aluminium rabbit ears on top. Vehicles were further adorned with a sign saying 'Hop-a-Bus'.

These motorized Easter bunnies pulled in thousands of extra travellers a week for the 5p ride. The rabbit motif was chosen in preference to grasshoppers, kangaroos, crickets and frogs, because according to the system's director of marketing, Mr Jerry Johnson, people find it easier to identify with rabbits.

And while most people found the whole idea refreshing and funny, Jerry reported that some thought it was not sophisticated enough.

One woman, in particular, complained that it was nothing more than a promotion for *Playboy* magazine and a promiscuous life-style.

.   .   .

In 1982, it was said that so many people dodged bus fares in Moscow that 3 new buses could be bought per week with the lost revenue.

One Comrade Dobrushin was enlisted to look into the matter and he concluded that the city's tough, aggressive female ticket inspectors were causing the problem. These women were forced to travel in pairs because they were so often assaulted. The reason for the violence could be linked to the fact that they took an extra-special interest in checking tickets, because they gained one-fifth of every on-the-spot fine.

Comrade Dobrushin didn't mince his words when describing his colleagues. They were 'rough, hooligan, ex-prostitute types', he said, displaying the kind of customer relations that would put BR to shame.

. . .

Queue-barging at bus stops became such a problem in 1975 that London Transport produced a poster campaign to discourage what they described as 'queue vandalism'.

Numerous ways of jumping the queue were identified, but some of the favourites included:

People who rushed to read the bus information at the front of the queue and forgot to go back. When the bus arrived they would hop on board.

The young athlete who sprinted from the back of the queue to board the bus with a flying leap, while less agile members of the queue were left standing.

Then there were the folk who would edge up the queue by pretending to look in a shop window or at the sky. By the time they had finished looking, they had moved a good few places.

And not forgetting those who never actually joined the queue but merely lingered on its edges. When the bus arrived, they would dart forward and climb on.

Next came the bully groups, often young men who would arrive in a bunch of 3 or 4. Their demeanour made it clear to the rest of the passengers that when the bus came they would most certainly be on it.

The real collector's item among queue-jumping had to be the experience of one veteran traveller. He remembered the day the queue dissolved into chaos when one passenger got on the bus and for no reason at all, called the conductor a pig.

. . .

One London bus conductor, exasperated by persistent fare-dodging, compiled a list of the most popular ruses.

The first was Hopping Hilda, named after a woman who caught buses on the hop for years. These women would pull the old 'innocent' dodge. When the conductor called for fares, Hopping Hilda would rummage through her handbag. After getting more and more flustered she would then pretend to have come out without any money.

Woefully, she would ask the conductor what she should do. The conductor would tell her to leave her name and address and post the fare to the transport authority when she got home. Naturally, the money never arrived. Hopping Hilda simply used a different name every time and seemed to move house every week.

Then there were the bookworms who buried their heads in the latest novel, using an old ticket as a bookmark to make it look as though they had paid. As the conductor approached, the reader became more and more engrossed in the gripping tale. Russian novels were often employed to impress the conductor.

Next were the short-change artists. One conductor recalled an old woman, a regular on his bus, who used to think that seven halfpennies made up a four-penny fare. After weeks of making up the correct fare out of his own pocket, he decided to give her a lesson in mathematics, making her count every halfpenny into his hand. After that she used to pay in sixpences.

A less common but nevertheless exotic species was Ornithological 'Enery, who discovered a rare bird on the wing just as the conductor reached his seat. He would be so absorbed in the outside world that he hoped the conductor would not notice that he didn't have a ticket.

Burlington Bertie was the city gentleman who 'realized' after a few stops that he was on the 'wrong' bus, but he stayed on a few more stops just in case. Then he got off to catch another bus along the same route. These 'mistakes' would finally take him to his destination.

There was the party-time trick where a gang of youths would all rush down the stairs shouting that their friend behind them had the money. In the end there were no friends left to pay the fares.

Conductors reckoned that they had seen all the fare-evaders, bar one. That was the man who walked into a London bus depot, jumped on the first bus that caught his eye and drove it away.

. . .

In Bristol in 1987, the driver of a bus-load of shoppers explained to a man boarding that he did not have change for his £10 note and would the gentleman mind an IOU?

Unfortunately for driver Geoff Prideaux, the passenger did mind and in a flash of rage he grabbed Geoff's glasses and ran off with them.

Geoff, now rendered completely myopic, had to ring for relief which took 15 minutes to arrive. A spokesman for the Bristol Bus Company appealed charitably for the smartly dressed man in his twenties to come forward – to collect his change.

. . .

In 1991, bus and train chiefs were told to leave their company cars at home and travel to work using public transport. To make sure that the chiefs complied with this ruling, they were asked to submit reports about cleanliness, staff attitudes and time-keeping.

The directive was issued by Centro, the West Midlands body which plans and finances local services. The aim was to reduce pollution and congestion on the roads. It was also to combat the criticism that the company cars were bought out of poll tax receipts for the very executives who were encouraging the public to make more use of the bus and train services.

Six executives hit by the directive had a further shock. The company was contemplating scrapping company cars altogether and issuing bus and train passes as part of the director's salary.

. . .

A free-travel perk offered to London policemen was given a thumbs-down by the 20,000-strong Metropolitan Police Federation.

London Transport's concession of free travel for policemen on or off duty was rejected as a clever attempt to get free policing on public transport.

. . .

Bus crews in Georgia in the days of the USSR once carried 435 passengers in one day and recorded the sale of just one ticket. The remaining 434 fares were pocketed. Moscow employed a notably thorough measure to combat this form of creative accounting – the death penalty.

. . .

In Moscow in 1972, bus conductors were largely abolished in favour of cumbersome ticket-dispensing machines: plastic and metal money-boxes with a roll of tickets which the customer operated for himself after dropping his coin in the slot.

This system caused a fair amount of public irritation, because there was always a crowd round the money-box which was placed inconveniently close to the entrance, and naturally was slow and inefficient. To overcome the problem posed by this technological improvement, a typically Russian compromise evolved – that is to say, one that caused the most misery and inconvenience possible. Henceforth the people at the back of the bus would pass their money forward, hand by hand, to the person nearest the machine, who then bought the tickets for the whole bus. The poor person nearest the box became, in effect, an unpaid conductor.

You Can't Do That There 'Ere

HOWEVER ANARCHIC AND freewheeling transport networks may appear, they are always underpinned by a morass of legislation, rules and regulations. It's not that they want to be laden with bureaucracy, but that they have to be. Or do they? We introduce this section on commuting law with what is probably our favourite getting-to-work story of all. Like so many astonishing things, it comes – of course – from Moose Jaw, Saskatchewan, in the Canadian mid-west.

. . .

In 1970, little Moose Jaw was in the grip of a commuting nightmare. The problem concerned pedestrians, more specifically the fact that they kept bumping into one another.

It is very important at this stage in the story to dismiss any cynical thought that Moose Jaw must have been a quiet sort of town for the occasional sidewalk mishap to have become a civic crisis. If the people of Moose Jaw deemed it a problem, who are we to say it was not? Something had to be done, and on 4 January, it was. The council passed a law making it mandatory to walk on the right-hand side of the pavement. Failure to do so could mean a fine of up to $100 or 30 days in jail.

It cannot be said that the ordinance was passed without controversy at that fateful evening council meeting. Alderman Gordon Pritchard, for one, described the move as ridiculous. He fumed that it would now be impossible, for example, to enter a building at the corner of Fairford and Main Streets if he happened to be walking north on Main Street. 'I would have to go all the way round the block first,' he said. Even stepping out to get a sandwich or a coffee could mean circumnavigating an entire city block if one were to keep within the new walking laws.

But Moose Jaw by-law 2423 went ahead all the same, signed by the mayor, Mr Pascoe, the city clerk, Mr Botting, and the city solicitor, Mr Dickinson. In a stirring speech in defence of the by-law, Alderman Mrs Raynell Andreychuk, its mover, said, 'If anyone was to stand on a cross-walk and watch the people crossing, sometimes six or seven abreast, one would wonder if they knew how to walk.'

By-law 2423 did not get off to a wholly terrific start. As a present city official recalled, 'A lot of ridicule was heaped upon the law. Two solicitors on the council considered it unenforceable. On the first morning, people actually made light of it. We had people on the sidewalks wearing helmets and giving hand signals. It wasn't a real success.'

On 9 April 1984, by-law 2423 was laid to rest. As a measure of its legislative excellence, not a single charge was laid under it in its 13-year life. And what happened to Alderman Andreychuk?

When last we heard, she was one of the most senior judges in Canada. And quite rightly, too.

. . .

Luciano Ruggiero, a quiet, middle-aged employee in a sugar factory, decided to take on the Italian government over their policy of reserving blocks of seats on trains for members of parliament. Signor Ruggiero complained that many lire-paying passengers had to stand next to empty seats that were reserved for 'honourable senators and deputies'.

Even when there were no such dignitaries around, the *hoi polloi* were not allowed to use them because the personnel on the railways had been instructed to keep them free in case an 'honourable' turned up.

One day, returning from the Italian Riviera to Genoa, Signor Ruggiero occupied a deputy's seat, and continued to sit there even when the conductor ordered him to move. The conductor, acting under government regulations, wrote out a court summons. The court fined Signor Ruggiero but he refused to pay.

Three months later an appeal court, obviously comprised of ordinary travellers, quashed the fine, saying that it was no crime to sit in a deputy's seat. But the public prosecutor appealed against this decision. The Chiavari appeal court heard the case for the second time and again upheld Ruggiero's acquittal. The prosecutor then swore to take the matter to Italy's highest tribunal, the Court of Cassation.

In spite of the dogged behaviour of the officials, Ruggiero won the case and became the hero of all Italian travellers.

. . .

In 1970, the passengers on board a local Terenove train in Italy protested about the filthy state of the carriages. They disembarked at the station and sat in front of the engine until the police broke them up an hour later. In the same year, another group of 400 passengers took ill treatment lying down. They lay across the tracks near Turin and held up trains for seven hours. Their protest was sparked by a guard who tried to make a season-ticket holder pay extra for travelling first class when there were no other seats.

. . .

In 1980, passengers caught singing on Italian trains faced fines. The crackdown was designed to deter English soccer hooligans, and to bar songs and choirs on board. Offenders faced maximum penalties of £250 or two months in gaol.

The fines apart, guards were ordered to remove any singers at the next stop. A spokesman said: 'Naturally these new get-tough measures will hit everyone, including such people as British soccer fans who come to Italy to cheer on their teams. If they win, they'll just have to control their emotions until they're out of Italy. There must be no singing. We're sorry – but that's the law.'

.   .   .

Since 1 December 1980, passengers on Italian trains are not permitted to open the window 'unless they have the permission of all the passengers'.

.   .   .

The Italian railways ordered a woman who carried two goldfish in a jamjar to pay £4 for their fares. The fish set off on the journey from Rome to Cassino, carried in the jar by Carmela Tiseo, and were quite happy until the ticket collector insisted that they came in the category of beasts weighing up to 25 kg.

Signorina Tiseo told him that the regulation was stupid, and when given the demand for payment commented: 'To think that even a Christian only pays £1.50 from Rome to Cassino.'

.   .   .

An ambulance racing to the scene of an accident on a French motorway was halted when a toll attendant told the driver to pay up like everyone else. The collector at the Bandol toll, near Toulon, told the ambulance driver to 'drop in your five-franc piece like everyone else and you can go through'. The driver, incensed, became involved in a fierce row. It ended when a fire engine, summoned on the ambulance's radio, smashed down the toll barrier, allowing the ambulance a free route through.

. . .

Ah Chong used to own a Chinese laundry in Brooklyn. Taking the Subway one day, he suffered a heart attack. Passengers around him begged the driver to stop, so that medical assistance could be found. The driver refused, saying that he would radio ahead for help. Half an hour and 13 stations later, passengers were still shouting and many were crying as nothing had happened, except the demise of Mr Chong.

The driver explained later that he had a wife and four children and daren't risk the sack by breaching regulations. Transport police along the route explained that they had not heard the train's emergency horn as it passed them.

. . .

Lincolnshire police carried out a full-scale investigation into a one-legged driver who had been issued with a licence to drive an unmodified car thirty-eight years before. Since the man's leg had been amputated, he used a walking stick to work the pedals as he pulled away in traffic.

Nearly 500 passengers were stranded for six hours when their HS225 train struck overhead lines in Bedfordshire. They sat there for the entire time without heating and with no food. Catering staff refused to re-open the buffet, claiming they had already done their stocktaking.

· · ·

A Chinese judge in Canton deals with fare dodgers on the buses by driving them 25 miles out of town and leaving them to walk home.

· · ·

Jake Mangle-Wurzle, a self-confessed eccentric, was caught trying to race BMWs and juggernauts while riding his motorcycle on the M25.

Jake, 52, and his dog – riding in a basket on the back of the bike – were competing with other motorists on a stretch of the motorway near St Albans, Hertfordshire, when the police stopped them.

Jake's motorcycle was not exactly designed for speed. It had a fan on the front, which Jake claimed was a 'pedestrian repellent', and a metal pole with an amber builder's light on the end protuding from the back, which was designed as a lightning conductor, in case of storms.

There was also a washing line gaily flapping across the top of the bike on which Jake and his dog dried their underwear.

Despite Jake's protestations that he was not driving a dangerous vehicle, the police disagreed and he was charged with reckless driving. However, when Jake's case came up, the magistrates simply laughed him out of court.

. . .

In 1989, the Pope told members of the Italian Automobile Club that to speed was to sin. Bringing morals to motoring, the Pope told the drivers that they would have to answer to God for their bad driving. He said motorists had a 'moral and religious' duty to drive safely and would face the ultimate court if they endangered lives or even 'ignored road security regulations'.

. . .

Council workers in Saddleworth, Greater Manchester, put up a sign directing traffic to Saddleworth station. The only problem was that the sign pointed in the wrong direction. But the error didn't matter too much anyway, because the station had been closed for 25 years.

. . .

In 1991, Lord Longford, aged 85, impatient to get back to his country mansion, was none too pleased to be ordered off his train due to engineering works. Carrying heavy baggage, he was herded onto a waiting bus along with other grumbling passengers. However, the Lord brightened somewhat when the bus drew up at a stop just outside his home in Hurst Green, East Sussex. With surprising alacrity, the octogenarian grabbed his cases and attempted to disembark, only to be told: 'Not here you don't. This is not a bus – it's a train.'

. . .

Taxi-drivers in Germany were left to fume in silence a few years ago after a new law was passed to prevent them from talking to their fares. And as if that wasn't insult enough, smoking and listening to the radio were also banned in the interests of road safety.

One taxi driver commented, 'They're not going to tell me to keep my mouth shut', while another pronounced the verdict 'idiocy'.

Under the ruling, drivers could only converse with a passenger in order to establish the route and destination. Infringements of the law meant a fine. The drivers argued that conversation was part of the expected service and one veteran added 'The more you talk, the bigger the tip.'

. . .

A proud German father was spotted on a busy road, operating the foot pedals while his eight-year-old son sat on his lap and steered the car.

. . .

When the traffic police came on duty in the Dutch town of Eindhoven, motorists and passers-by cheered them heartily. For on the previous day, the town's police chief, fed up by complaints that his men were not smart enough, had invited 18 men from a local factory to direct the Friday night rush-hour traffic.

The gallant 18 did their best to untangle the mess caused by 15,000 cyclists, 10,000 pedestrians and 1,000 cars. Standing on small raised platforms, they whistled, waved, pleaded and begged the traffic to be orderly, and ignored the constant stream of advice from onlookers.

The verdict afterwards seemed to be conclusive – the police weren't so bad after all. 'Never again. The blood is in my shoes and will stay there for hours,' said one of the stand-in traffic cops. A cyclist said, 'Give us the regulars – it took us twice as long to get home than usual.' And the police themselves said of the factory workers' effort: 'Not bad for amateurs, but what a lot of wasted energy.' Curiously, however, there hadn't been a single accident.

• • •

There was applause when Sark's parliament approved legislation to control the island's tractors.

Sark's famous ban on cars, motorcycles and even sit-on lawnmowers – a doctor who moved there just before the war was given permission to use his car only if a horse was attached to the front to pull the vehicle — did not extend to tractors, which were supposed to be used for agricultural purposes. More often than not, however, they were used to carry the shopping home or to meet someone at the harbour.

The 55 tractor owners on Sark had to apply for a licence from the road traffic committee. Those who had owned their tractors for more than five years automatically received a licence, but later owners had to convince the committee that the tractor was necessary for their business. Mrs Pat Falle, the committee chairman, said she hoped the new measures would reduce the numbers of tractors from 55 to about 47, and then there would be another decrease as the existing tractors wore out. In fact, by 1992, there were still 50 working tractors on Sark.

The island is a traffic cop's nightmare, even if there are no cars. There is, for example, a speed limit of 10 m.p.h. — and of 5 m.p.h. by the harbour. However, as tractors are incapable of taking a steep hill at only 5 m.p.h., theoretically every tractor breaks the law every day.

Then there is the question of Sark's unique two-way one-way street, on which cycles can go in one direction and tractors, horses and so on in the other. Finally, there is some official haziness about whether Sark drives on the right or left. Tradition has it that French visitors cycle their hired bikes on the right, the rest on the left. The locals ride on whichever side is sheltered from the wind – but prefer to go down the middle.

. . .

A pretty bus conductress in Russia got a kiss from
her driver and the sack from her employer in 1988.
When Tamara Shikanova gave her fiancé, Yegor
Kostenko, his lunchtime sandwiches, he thanked
her with a hug and a kiss in front of the other
passengers.

The passengers themselves didn't mind a bit, but
another driver, Anna Volodina, did. So Altruistic
Anna complained to her bosses that Yegor's act
was 'unworthy of the profession'.

The complaint was passed on to the trade union
committee who agreed that Tamara and Yegor had
'compromised the honour of their collective'.
Tamara was sacked; Yegor got away with a fine.

. . .

Bournemouth's bus conductor KK 46793 had never stopped his bus so that a passenger could enjoy
the view until 1970, when one Pheroze Minvalla
got on board.

Mr Minvalla, a civil servant, was a passenger
riding-to-rule in protest at the busmen's work-to-
rule. As the bus set off from Bournemouth, Mr
Minvalla announced that he wanted to pay his fare
in accordance with Section 5 of the rule book. He
then produced a bank note to pay his 40p fare.

'Are you the conductor?' he asked. Uniformed

conductor KK 46793 replied, 'No, I'm a lorry driver.' 'Well then,' retorted Mr Minvalla, 'where is your authorization from the Traffic Commissioners?' KK 46793 could hardly believe his ears. After asking several more exacting questions, Mr Minvalla seemed satisfied and accepted his ticket.

But he wasn't going to leave it there. Still complying to the statutory orders and regulations covering public service vehicles, Mr Minvalla asked for the bus to pull up at a request stop. He didn't want to get off, but there again the rule book says he doesn't have to. Perhaps Mr Minvalla and KK 46793 are still there.

. . .

A driver who misread his timetable left 40 passengers and his bus on double yellow lines at the side of the road, while he walked off to the nearest depot.

Pulling up and taking his cash-bag, the driver disappeared into the smoke, leaving bemused passengers to figure out what was going on. As they were sitting there, a police patrolman got on board, told them that the bus was parked illegally and slapped a parking ticket on the windscreen.

. . .

Girls riding the buses in Rome were warned that if they made themselves eye-poppingly attractive they could be fined.

Bus conductors were appointed 'morality' watchers in a bizarre move by officials of Rome's public transport system. They resurrected a 1946 law, which had never been enforced, that made indecency on the buses an offence.

Making himself quite clear, a transport spokesman said: 'The girls we are after are those who wear miniskirts right up to their backsides.' Another bus driver agreed, saying: 'Foreign tourists dress in a disgusting manner. They just ask for trouble.' His younger colleague, however, said he would not fine any pretty young girl, especially if she was 'scantily dressed'.

. . .

In 1932, a new fleet of three-decker buses was unveiled in Rome. They had a special compartment for dogs.

. . .

Bus drivers in Rio de Janeiro who were caught speeding used to be sent to the penal colony on Ihla Grande Island. In one year alone, 17 busmen were arrested in the city and accused of training beetles to steal plastic tokens out of fare boxes. They were estimated to have taken £46,000. Seven of the beetles held by the police unfortunately died of starvation, so were unable to give evidence.

. . .

A drunk driver, Frank Leibling, was sentenced to 100 hours of community service work at Rochester Zoo in New York. Arriving there by bus, Frank was given a broom and asked to clean out the elephant pens. After a hard day's work, Frank went to catch the bus home, but the driver refused to let him on board, saying that the smell would offend other passengers.

. . .

In the drop-off zone at Deerfield Commuter Station in Illinois there is a road sign to remind drivers that kissing is prohibited. It is an ordinary sign with a couple kissing and a red stripe through the centre to emphasize the point.

. . .

Male cab drivers in Los Angeles are no longer allowed to wear skirts to work. A new code designed to stop cross-dressing by transvestite cabbies is reinforced by a $600 fine for those not adhering to it.

. . .

If you are frequently caught speeding, then consider a move to California. The state has over 400 licensed schools for teaching road-safety to drivers who commit minor travel offences. But if the thought of these schools conjures up a dowdy image of a put–U–right place, then think again.

There is the Lettuce Amuse U Laff-&-Learn traffic school where drivers can giggle through an eight-hour safety class, taught by professional comics. Perhaps the biggest laugh of all is that as a result a driver's offence is kept off the records.

Other choices are the It Wasn't My Fault traffic school, the Magic Entertainers School and the Rose Robin traffic school for chocoholics.

In 1990, 1.2 million of the state's 19.5 million drivers opted to attend schools at a cost of from £8 to £18 a day plus a £12 court fee. Offenders must also pay their traffic fines.

Those offenders with a sense of humour failure, or who don't harbour a fetish for chocolate, can opt for a conventional class where ex-policemen teach them where they went wrong.

However, the California Department of Motor Vehicles did refuse to license one proposed school. It planned to teach the eight-hour course on a bus returning from Las Vegas where the offenders would have spent a good few hours gambling. 'Traffic school is not meant to be entirely fun,' claimed a department spokesman.

· · ·

A British driver in Italy was once stopped in the middle of a traffic jam by a policeman. The policeman demanded £15 for an offence that he had just dreamt up. The man tried to explain that he was British and didn't understand what the policeman was talking about.

The policeman then relented and asked for £7.50. The driver continued to protest for another ten minutes, by which time all the cars behind him were honking their horns.

Finally the two men agreed on the sum of £5, and the policeman, safely pocketing his booty, sauntered across to the nearest bar leaving the traffic to sort itself out.

. . .

When new parking restrictions were adopted in Rome, a crowd of passers-by applauded when a police breakdown lorry towed away a limousine three times its size. They clapped even louder as the owner appeared and had to hop in a taxi to chase it.

. . .

Traffic chief Antonio Pala, incensed at the failure of his elaborate suburban parking scheme, once opened the whole of Rome for 48 hours in a bid to *increase* car chaos.

The city's 650,000 motorists were invited to take to the streets, with no risk of being fined, for two whole days. All parking restrictions were waived in the hope that the ensuing chaos might make drivers more tolerant of on-the-spot parking fines.

Chief Antonio sat back and waited for motorists to hang themselves. 'There will be double parking and triple parking. Streets will be blocked,' he said gleefully. 'We hope it will be an absolute nightmare.'

. . .

In Sydney, 150 lorry drivers once went on strike because they said that their firm was paying them too much money. The extra cash was incentive payments which they just did not want. Union officials reported that the scheme bought bickering, rudeness and traffic breaches.

. . .

Nine knitting matrons caused havoc in Nelson, New Zealand, when they stopped the demolition of a railway. Nelson, a quiet, sleepy town, has the country's highest sunshine record and its shortest railway spur – to Glenhope, 60 miles away.

The government, long concerned about mounting losses on this line, finally decided to demolish it. On Monday morning, the demolition gangs went in to start work. On the Tuesday, 55-year-old Mrs Ruth Page and eight supporting housewives drove to the scene, 40 miles from Nelson. They set down cushions on the rails, and sat there knitting and gossiping.

Every morning for a week, they were driven out by taxi – supplied free – and took up their positions. Sometimes they had picnics, sometimes they made tea. Sympathizers supplied them with ice-cream. Each time the demolition gang moved to pick the next rail, the women went on talking and knitting. If the workmen switched to break up a building, Mrs Page and her group upped needles, went into the building and sat on the floor.

News reached Wellington, the capital, and a posse of departmental chiefs took a train to the scene. Halfway there, they came across Mrs Page and her group, sitting pretty and knitting furiously. So the department chiefs went back.

The following day someone cut the telephone wires and interfered with the water supply of the township where the demolition gang worked. The Prime Minister called this 'an act of sabotage' and ordered police action. So an inspector, a sergeant and a constable approached the sitting knitters and warned them against trespass, saying that if they continued they would be taken into custody.

At this threat, Mrs Page ceased knitting for a minute and said very politely, 'We watched our men do conventional lawful things without results; now we are doing forceful things. We want the whole of New Zealand to know we will be run over by trains if necessary.'

Shortly after this, the matrons were charged with trespass and obstruction. While waiting to enter Nelson Magistrates' Court, they re-arranged the curtains at the police station and one of them darned socks for a bachelor constable. The nine were remanded on bail.

. . .

Taxi drivers in Stockholm were taken to court after police complaints about their 'irregular clothing'. Three taxi drivers were accused of offences against the regulations concerning attire.

The taxi companies had requested the regulations after their members were found at the wheel in brown-striped shirts, polka dot ties and without a driver's cap. This sort of 'slovenly behaviour' was liable to result in a fine. Swedish taxi drivers are supposed to wear uniform caps, white, light-blue or grey shirts and black ties.

. . .

In 1989, French police caught Finance Minister Michel Charasse speeding on the motorway. But because of the delicacy of the situation, the radar pictures showing the Minister driving at 78 m.p.h. – 30 m.p.h. over the limit – were diplomatically thrown away.

The French Minister was furious about this, however, and complained to the Police Chief of Paris about his preferential treatment. He threatened to create a storm unless he was taken to court, fined and banned from driving.

. . .

La Rentrée is the time when holidaying Parisians return home and is a nightmare for traffic police. The trouble starts at the Périphérique, the notorious 22-mile loop that circles Paris. On this road

20 per cent of fatalities are caused by heart attacks. Capitaine Jean Simon, head of the 240-strong police force which patrols the 'Péri', as it is more fondly dubbed, recalls incidents of motorists pulling chain saws out of their boots to dismantle crash barriers, in an effort to escape.

. . .

In 1989, an official clamp-down on parking in the centre of Paris created havoc. Businesses reported record absenteeism, and two executives became embroiled in a ramming duel while fighting over the last legal parking space.

A traffic policeman said that within an hour of his going on duty, a woman had fainted in his arms after seeing her car towed away, another had hit him with her handbag, while several others had threatened him with violence.

During this period of increased police vigilance, the number of cars being towed away per day doubled to about 750. But the drivers were not the only ones to feel the brunt of the new measures. Police officers themselves reported an increase in the painful 'parking fine finger' as a result of writing too many tickets in an awkward or stressful position.

. . .

Brussels City Council decided that people over 75

years old would get traffic priority – if they carried yellow walking sticks.

. . .

In 1989, a new motorway between Shanghai and Jiading in China caused problems for motorists who hitherto had been accustomed to a top speed of 20 m.p.h.

In one week a total of 61 vehicles unable to cope with life in the third lane broke down, while another 83 drivers lost their licences for speeding. These drivers were caught doing 'as much as 50 m.p.h.' claimed the deputy traffic director, Fu Zhiming, who said that the increase in the speed limit to 38 m.p.h. had obviously 'gone to their feet'.

But it wasn't only the drivers who fell foul of the new motorway. Some 700 pedestrians were also booked – for crossing it. The only person who seemed to benefit was a travel agent who offered a half-day tour to 'view this thrilling roller-coaster'.

. . .

Peking in the 1970s was the only city in the world where it was actually the rule to turn across the road in front of a bus and against a red light. Traffic lights changed from green to red in an instant, and an amber light meant turn left.

There was no Highway Code, so the only recommended way to drive was slowly, sounding your horn continually. Moreover, to obtain a Chinese driving licence, a foreigner had to undergo a medical examination, the key factor of which was blood pressure. But since the average Chinese person's blood pressure is substantially lower than that of a European, many healthy people found themselves grounded.

Eventually, Peking's traffic chaos was blamed (along with everything else) on the 'The Gang of Four', who had in turn been engaged in an attack on the authority of the police and the judiciary. A 'sinister ace general' at the Peking police headquarters was reputed to have deliberately neglected to train police for traffic duties. Any policeman who tried to exert his authority was in danger of being denounced as a 'Right deviationist' exercising 'bourgeois dictatorship' over the proletariat. We advise that you try that argument with your local traffic warden.

• • •

A young gentleman from Essex who had indulged in some serious liquid refreshment caught the train home and overshot his destination by several stations. With his brain in a state of disrepair, he then tried to pick his way home back along the track. The next thing he heard was an oncoming train – so he promptly lay down. The result of this rash action was later disclosed: 'The train passed clean over him, not a bolt of it touched his body and he continued on his way unhurt,' said a British Rail spokesman, who admittedly sounded a little proud of the train.

.   .   .

After a spate of complaints from first-class travellers about second-class ticket holders sitting in first class, British Rail took some unusual precautions. They dressed a number of their ticket inspectors in pinstripe suits, briefcases and brollies and handed them a copy of *The Times*, the possession of which is guaranteed not to arouse suspicion in fellow commuters.

On the first day of the ruse, eight of these incognito inspectors nabbed over fifty commuters for travelling in first class without the appropriate ticket.

.   .   .

Michael Toole, 24, arrived five minutes early for the last train, the 1.10 a.m. from Oxford to Banbury. A red-faced porter told him that in fact the train had already left, but promised that British Rail would get him home somehow. Michael, expecting a taxi, was amazed when BR provided a 117-ton, 100-m.p.h. diesel locomotive crewed by two amused drivers. Twenty-five minutes and twenty-two seconds later the VIP one-passenger-special drew up in Banbury. 'We aim to please,' purred BR. 'Regulations say that if a passenger is stranded and it's our fault, we have to do something about it. The 1.10 did pull out early so we gave the young man the full works.'

. . .

Another example of dogmatic pragmatism led the elected officials of a transport society to be Herman the cat, Polly the parrot and an unnamed goldfish. The cat's owner, Mr Michael Land, was the moving spirit behind a plan to run buses from Brighton to London at a fraction of the price of the rail fare. To avoid the inevitable objections from British Rail about undercutting services, Mr Land made the family cat, Herman, the official chairman of the Society For the Preservation of Old Buildings. The Society is part of the established Brighton Line Commuters Association, of which Mr Land is the chairman. He felt that since BR would have objected to the Traffic Commissioners about his plan to run coaches, he did not want any human element involved in the writs and paperwork that were likely to ensue.

Alongside Herman, or Chairman Miaow as he is also known, stands Polly the parrot who is unlikely to drop anyone in it since she can't speak a word.

. . .

Pulling the communication cord on a Russian train is not dismissed lightly. At one time, offenders could expect to face 12 months' 'corrective labour' or a two-year stint in gaol. If unauthorized cord-pulling caused an accident, the sentence could be increased to eight years. The measure came after an increase in train-hopping, which is known in Russia as 'going with the breeze'. This involved jumping on to a passing train, usually a goods train, and applying the guard's emergency brake when the train reached a particular spot. This spot was usually outside the passenger's town, or if he was lucky, his house. Over a period of 6 months on one branch of the Moscow–Kuibyshev line, 1,259 such 'passengers' were caught by the authorities. Over three months 382 trains were forced to stop illegally – a rate of one every six hours.

. . .

Unlike British Rail, Indian railways make a profit. And it would be even larger, say Indian officials, if all the passengers paid their fares. But well over 6 million don't.

Trains would be faster too, say the officials, if commuters didn't pull the communication cord unnecessarily. But they do – about 100,000 times a year. Indeed, pulling the alarm chain, along with ticketless travel and assaulting railway staff, were at one time India's national sport. Alarm chains were pulled an average of 118 times a day. Pulling the communication cord in India is not perceived as simply a method of stopping a train in an emergency, but also as a political protest. Chains are pulled in dissatisfaction over linguistic policies, increases in the cost of living or the government's policy of resettling refugees.

Yet despite the evidence against them, passengers have great respect for India's 'Iron Horses'. In remote areas, some people still believe that steam engines are gods which control their destinies.

Indian midwives, however, are slightly shrewder when it comes to trains. They sell used train tickets for women in labour to chew on. 'Express' tickets fetch the most. They guarantee a quick birth.

. . .

India's Central Railway once realized £130,000 during a three-month period in fines from passengers caught travelling without a ticket. In the state of Bihar, ticketless travel is especially popular, and foreigners on trains there often find themselves the only ticket holders. Members of the Ticketless Travellers' Association, which existed for many years, paid an annual subscription fee of 7s 6d which assured them free legal aid if they got caught. The president, a gentleman from Calcutta, claims to have travelled all his life on Indian railways without a ticket. He says he was never found out.

Ramchandra Kashiram, an Indian peasant from Bihar, was not so lucky. He ended up in gaol for 29 years after being caught on the railways without a ticket. Unfortunately, officials lost his papers and so he was never called to trial. Two civil-liberties lawyers got to hear of his case – just after Kashiram had been released.

. . .

In New Delhi about 1,200 conductors and drivers of trams and buses went to work clad in only vest and pants. They were campaigning for increased wages and free uniforms.

. . .

Employees of the state-owned railway in Bhavnagar, Gujarat, celebrated May Day with a display of self-criticism. They paraded with an effigy representing red tape, which was then duly burned.

. . .

Spanish railway authorities once sent an indignant note to a man who owned a parrot. The piercing whistles of this pretty polly, they maintained, had frequently been sending trains out of the nearby station ahead of schedule. The parrot, belonging to the owner of the station hotel at Cestona near San Sebastian, had apparently been disrupting timetables for months. The authorities instructed the owner to keep the pretty disruptive polly safely locked away.

. . .

In 1986 two Tokyo railway workers were made to clean toilets for a couple of months as a punishment. Their crime had been to grow moustaches. The two workers, Rikio Anzai, 40, and Makoto Kikuchi, 37, took the management of the state railways to court and demanded their old jobs back. Their argument was that 'There is nothing strange about facial hair in Japan and management has no justification to claim that passengers dislike seeing a moustachioed railwayman.'

The state railways rule book says nothing about facial hair, but one personnel manager said he believed that it gave passengers 'a bad impression', betokening a casual, easy-going approach to life.

The main objection seemed to be that men with facial hair stand out from their colleagues, and this is seen as detracting from discipline and efficiency in Japanese firms where conformity is highly prized. As the old Japanese adage goes, 'The nail that sticks out gets hammered down.'

. . .

Buskers on New York's Subway were once as unscheduled as the trains, but in 1987 the Metropolitan Transportation Authority began to institutionalize the free music service. Buskers were invited to audition for their prestigious subterranean spots. 'Auditioning to play in the Subway!' said one musician. 'Ain't New York something?'

On the first day of auditions, however, 63 acts turned up including a bagpiper, a man who played the trumpet and keyboards at the same time, and another who played on his home-made 'Cajun cello' which turned out to be an instrument comprised of old boxes.

'The Subway is not a bad gig,' mused the leader of a jazz band called 'Chicken's Wings'. 'We sometimes make more money in the stations than we do in a club.' James Grasek, a violinist who augments his professional career with performances on Lexington Avenue at 23rd Street, said, 'People are surprised, delighted and always appreciative, and the nice thing is that you can count on delays which makes for a large captive audience.'

5

That Doesn't Happen Every Day

LET'S FACE IT, commuting is almost a synonym for routine, repetitive and dreary. Most people go a lifetime without anything remotely interesting or unusual happening on the way to work or en route to anywhere else.

But then again, the oddest things do happen . . .

. . .

The assistant station master at Campiglia Marittima, Italy, Elvio Bartlettani, was sitting in his office one day when a dog calmly jumped out of a goods train. The dog nosed its way across the level crossing, found its way into Elvio's office and went to sleep. Realizing that the dog must have travelled a long way, Elvio gave it some soup, called it Lampo and allowed it to stay.

It transpired that Lampo's favourite pastime was not chasing rabbits but travelling on trains. One morning when the Rome express arrived Lampo wandered aboard. Arriving in Rome, he negotiated a train back to Campiglia at the end of the day.

Every few days, Lampo would hitch a lift on a train and travel across Italy. He got to know the trains with kitchen staff who would give him scraps, loved slow trains and shunned goods trains. His favourite journey was apparently the one from Campiglia to Pisa.

An agitated station official from Rome once telephoned Elvio to ask what he should do with the travelling hound. 'Nothing,' replied Elvio calmly.

Lampo travelled thousands of miles across Italy in this fashion. When he was banished by official order from Campiglia Marittima and taken 300 miles away, he returned via Rome, having changed trains a number of times, only the next day.

Lampo eventually died on the railway he loved – by mistiming a through express when he was using the level crossing.

. . .

Railwaymen in Sydney passed the hat round for their best-known fare-dodger, who landed up in hospital after an ill-judged jump for a train. Every day for ten years, Boxer the dog made the journey from one end of Sydney to the other, and every day he made the same last-minute dash to board his train.

Regular fare-payers travelling the same route used to feed him, and some said he lived the life of Riley. Unfortunately one day Boxer leapt a second too late, hit the automatic doors and fell down between the train and the platform.

Railwaymen promptly had a whip round and raised enough for Boxer's veterinary hospital fees.

Kent commuter Jackie Poole missed the journey to work so badly when she went on holiday to Canada that she sent her fellow travellers a postcard. She addressed it to 'George Penn and Co., Noisy crowd opposite the entrance waiting for the 7.29 a.m. fast to Cannon Street, Herne Bay Station'. The station porter made the final delivery.

. . .

Railway police at Victoria station found a man who had travelled 30 miles to London from Maidstone on a train's buffers. Rail staff found him staggering around the platform with his clothes in shreds, having spent an hour and seven minutes whistling through several country stations and the whole of south London as a sort of figurehead. BR only called in the police after he failed to produce a ticket.

. . .

Commuter Michael Peachey of Epping, Essex, decided to wear a medieval suit of armour on the Central Line as a protest against overcrowding on rush-hour Underground trains. He was photographed solemnly reading the *Daily Telegraph* through his visor.

. . .

A train that left from platform 5 of Rome's central

station used to be known as the 'Hot Pants Express'. For as the train sped between Rome and Milan, a posse of girls sashayed down the aisles, wearing the latest summer fashions.

Passengers were shown everything from full-length skirts to hot pants, and at major stations the girls tripped off and gave an impromptu performance to those in the waiting rooms or along the platform.

The scheme, which had the backing of some of the best fashion houses in Italy, only involved specially chosen girls who were neither too tall nor too slim, so as not to alienate women passengers. An official said: 'We don't want absolute matchsticks – after all, one eats and drinks on trains.'

. . .

German Fräuleins on the Munich–Verona express were accused of organizing orgies on board the trains taking them to their holiday destinations. Ticket collectors and guards were reputed to turn a blind eye to the girls who got into the spirit early on by staging strip shows and wild parties. The girls were apparently so desperate for Latin lovers that one or two of them had attempted to seduce policemen by mistake.

Italian state railways said they would not wait for an investigation before taking action. They replaced many of their younger workers with distinctly older men, who, as the spokesman put it, 'will be immune from female temptations'.

A 35-year-old Turk boarded a train in Brussels to go on holiday. Some 20 of his friends and relatives came to see him off and to help him load his luggage onto the express.

He needed help, for his luggage weighed one and a half tons and was packed into 22 suitcases and 35 bulky parcels. These contained a Volkswagen car, stripped into parts, a washing machine, also broken down into bits and pieces, a refrigerator and, naturally, the kitchen sink.

The train had to be held up while the loading went on. The luggage filled the whole of one compartment and blocked the corridor of two carriages.

The Turk, on his way home to Istanbul, claimed that he was only carrying hand luggage.

. . .

In 1991, passengers at Charing Cross in London were alarmed to see a dead man being wheeled bolt upright through the station in mid rush-hour. The now former commuter had been running for the 5.49 p.m. to Greenwich and collapsed in the carriage. Despite the attentions of two doctors who happened to be on board, the man failed to recover.

He was taken from the train by the London Ambulance Service and trundled for the very last time across a busy concourse. One onlooker, Rachael Slip, said: 'What an undignified way to go.'

Tube passengers were trapped at London's Old Street station after the driver let them off by mistake. The station was officially closed for the two-day Christmas holiday.

More than a dozen passengers disembarked, but by the time they realized the station was locked, the train had already left.

Some time later, after the passengers had managed to alert the London Fire Brigade, an Underground spokesman said: 'We are very sorry about this.'

. . .

When W. J. Ham, aged 60, collapsed and died at the wheel of his number 90 bus in George Street, Richmond, Surrey, the local newspaper reported: 'Before collapsing he stopped the bus.'

. . .

Police had to apologize for wrongly identifying two sisters who had been killed while crossing a road in Surrey. Someone who claimed to know the pair well identified them, but got the wrong sisters. It was discovered that Mrs Doris Thurgate and her sister Marion were actually alive and well. They were in fact having lunch when a policeman telephoned to inform them that they had just passed on.

. . .

An advert in the personal column of a national newspaper which ran 'Nobleman's Genuine Venetian Gondola, in excellent condition, lying Thames, for sale', prompted Miss Joyce Whatley to write in.

She said that an Italian friend of hers had brought it over from Venice in 1932 and had taken her on its maiden voyage on the Thames, gliding towards Maidenhead.

The gondolier was, of course, a real Italian, but he had reckoned without the strong currents of the Thames. The gondola proved to be too heavy to be managed with a single oar, and the trip ended with Miss Whatley and the Italian clinging to the bank just above a weir.

. . .

Heading for Chertsey, Surrey, a driver looked in his car mirror and noticed, as you would, a train thundering along behind him and catching up fast. Slamming on his brakes, the motorist swerved and flung open his car door to escape. But the door hit a live wire, and vanished in a puff of smoke. The train halted a few feet away and the driver leapt out of the car unhurt. It was now that the commuter discovered what he was already beginning to suspect – that he had taken a wrong turn, and was driving along the electrified railway line from London.

. . .

Another car commuter on his way home from Wellingborough, Northamptonshire, managed to avoid train lines, but did get an unexpected tap on his shoulder while he was minding his own business at traffic lights. He turned to find himself looking straight into the jaws of a five-foot-tall Himalayan black bear that had somehow found its way into the back of his estate car. The driver punched it deftly on the nose and then drove to an RAC centre near Northampton. Here he shouted at the startled patrolman on duty the only thing a man in his position could shout – 'Help, there's a bear in my car.'

. . .

Traffic on the M1 motorway was disrupted when hundreds of pairs of frilly knickers fell off the back of a lorry. Police patrolman Tony de Vos became aware of the problem when some of the lacy briefs flew over his car. Pulling over onto the hard shoulder, he collected about 150 pairs and then gave up.

Council workmen who rushed from their depot in Breaston, Notts, were only too happy to help clear the road. Predictably one of them was on hand to provide the kind of time-honoured quote that local newspapers expect of their victims: 'It was quite a frill.'

. . .

In 1992, a Berkshire tractor driver, Frederick Baden-Powell, was mistaken for a fox and shot at while driving after dark.

The man with the gun, Christopher Marshall, had been stalking foxes near Newbury and thought that the distant headlights of the tractor were the eyes of his prey, so had a blast at them. Fred was unhurt, but the tractor was damaged.

· · ·

In 1991, mysterious circles similar to those found in cornfields around the world were discovered in Tokyo's underground. These circles appeared in dust that had not been disturbed for a quarter of a century. Although smaller than crop circles, the metro circles appeared similarly symmetrical and often in linked patterns that excited scientists.

However, Professor Yoshi Hiko Ohtsuki, the scientist who revealed them, disappointed alien watchers by saying that the dust circles were caused by eddying currents of air, which were possibly electrically charged, and not by UFOs. What UFOs would have been doing in a Tokyo tunnel in the first place was never made clear – unless it was for the spacemen to learn a thing or two from the Japanese about efficient transport.

· · ·

Brian Inglis, in his book *Coincidences*, tells a story about the actor Anthony Hopkins. Hopkins was offered a part in the play *The Girl from Petrovka*. Wanting to be fully prepared for the role, the actor tried to get a copy of the novel by George Feifer, from which the play had been taken.

Despite scouring the whole of London, his search for the book was fruitless. Waiting to take the train home at Leicester Square, Hopkins noticed a book that had been left on a seat. It was a copy of Feifer's novel, full of helpful notes which had been scribbled in the margin.

When Hopkins later met the novelist, he learnt that a friend of the author, to whom Feifer had lent his own annotated copy, had lost it somewhere in London. It was the copy that Hopkins had found.

. . .

Brian Inglis, in *Coincidences*, also relates the case of one Andrew Hudson who was on the M1 being driven to Manchester by Mr Ian Jardin. As they approached the Watford Gap service area, Mr Jardin noticed that he was having trouble accelerating and pulled onto the hard shoulder to see what the problem was. Eventually he called the AA out and the two men were able to set off an hour and a half later.

Four months later Mr Hudson was driven past the same spot on the M1, this time by Dr Stephen Satterthwaite of British Steel. As the car passed the place where the original trouble had occurred, Mr Satterthwaite also began to have problems accelerating and again they pulled over and rang for assistance. Mr Hudson was waiting by the car for help to come when he saw a familiar car approaching. It was that of Mr Jardin.

. . .

Leo Bergmann, a garage mechanic, was fined £2,000 in Dusseldorf, Germany, for causing a traffic jam by inexplicably and unteutonically driving his Porsche in the middle of the road – at 22 m.p.h.

. . .

In 1979, there was a nasty outbreak of 'ghost drivers' on the motorways in West Germany. The 'ghosts' were motorists who drove the wrong way up crowded autobahns. Some of the ghosts were people who had just got mixed up at the last intersection, often foreigners not used to the roads. But there were reports of 'ghosts' being young joyriders who were playing 'chicken'. Their idea was to see who could drive up the motorway the wrong way for the longest time, without dying. The longest known 'record' was three hours.

. . .

Buenos Aires taxi driver Pedro Zardoras, 72, offered what could be described as probably the strangest cab service in the world. Whenever a passenger got into his taxi, he told them that his eyesight was really poor and that it would be safer all round if the passenger drove them both to the required destination. If the passenger agreed to do this, Zardoras would only charge half the fare.

. . .

A transport operator in the Australian port of Darwin went out of his way to hire a heavy drinker as a diesel mechanic. He placed an advertisement in the local paper offering £20 a week for a non-drinker but £36 for a heavy drinker – on the grounds that 'drinkers are better men and more efficient in the tropics'.

After sifting through the applicants, who replied by telephone, telegram or in person, the operator had to admit defeat. Only eight of the replies were genuine drinkers and most of those weren't mechanics.

He said sadly: 'I am frankly disappointed in Australian beer drinkers. They've let me down when I was trying to defend them.'

. . .

One musical car commuter was spotted in France playing a trumpet as he weaved in and out of heavy traffic in time to the music. But this was a veritably safe driver compared with a madman who in 1989 gave himself the exotic title of 'The Black Prince', and set off on a motorcycle from the Porte d'Italie to lap the Périphérique – the Paris ring-road – in just 9 minutes. His average speed was 144 m.p.h. The Prince boasted later that he would have made better time had it not been for the drag factor of the TV camera fitted to his helmet. His sponsors had insisted that he wore it.

. . .

In 1991 an amorous couple turned a normal train into a sleeper and caused havoc among commuters. The naked couple were found locked in an embrace on the floor of a first-class compartment, oblivious of both the world and the disgruntled commuters tutting through the window. Items of their clothing decorated the seats, and the windows had steamed up. One passenger, obviously a little more disgruntled than the others, pulled the communication cord, stopping the Reading to London breakfast train at Wokingham. Here a station worker, Brian Chance, was ceremoniously called in to uncouple the couple. Brian, a man of subtle means, said he had contemplated chucking a bucket of cold water over the duo, but refrained because 'it would make the carpets wet'. BR staff ordered the couple to get dressed and they were then taken to the parcels office to be interviewed by the police. A BR spokesman said that charges would not be laid because 'the couple had valid tickets for the journey'.

. . .

Another pair, obviously not unkeen on one another, put on an impromptu cabaret for a carriage full of City workers. But these businessmen took no exception to the pretty teenager seducing her boyfriend on the 8.52 p.m. from Waterloo to Guildford. In fact they clapped and cheered as the girl got underway. Shouting 'It's his birthday and this is his present!' the girl leapt agilely out of her leather skirt and red blouse and into the arms of her lover. The sexy show captivated the audience for a full seventeen minutes and only ended when the train drew into Surbiton, Surrey. Here the couple disappeared rapidly, the girl giggling, her companion grinning from ear to ear, and the commuters no doubt sad to see them go. And what did BR have to say on the matter – 'Well they didn't have much time, did they?' mused a spokesman.

. . .

When bus driver Angelo Teriuzzo splashed a group of people waiting at a bus stop in Milan, one of them chased the bus, grabbed him and took off his trousers. He was forced to drive back to the depot in his underwear.

. . .

Miami bus drivers once held a beach party for 15,000 customers to explain that it was not their fault that fares had increased by 5 cents. In an effort to win the support of the public, they raided the union kitty to provide a huge banquet consisting of 30,000 hot dogs, 45,000 soft drinks, 15,000 helpings of baked beans and a ton of chicken. Guests came straight from church in their Sunday best at the prospect of free food. The drivers themselves manned the 12 charcoal grills, while 8 bands, 10 rock groups and 12 church choirs played all day. After such huge effort and expense, it was still not clear whether the popularity of Miami's bus drivers had improved.

. . .

In 1987, a man stole a New York bus from its garage, picked up passengers and delivered them right to their doors, without charging them. It's worth noting, though, that when a New York bus is started without the proper procedures, an anti-theft device flashes 'Emergency – Call Police' on the computerized destination sign in front of the passengers. The man drove round for five hours without a single New Yorker responding.

. . .

A passenger waiting for a number 30 bus in Norwich watched it sail by because it was full. So he ran on to the next stop to catch it there. It was still full so he ran onto the next stop, then the next stop, and then the stop after that.

'Whichever stop I passed, he was there,' said the bemused bus driver, Mr Ray Appleyard.

It was only 8 stops later that the man finally crawled on board, red-faced and with just enough breath left to say that he was in a hurry and couldn't wait for the next bus.

The driver worked out that the passenger, who was wearing a hat and coat, had covered two and a half miles in nine and a half minutes, which is only 1 minute and 12 seconds slower than the world record.

A spokesman for the company said, 'The crews are keeping an eye out for him. They want to know who he is – to enter him for the Olympics.'

. . .

Richard Gerard from Plaistow, London, described how while managing his morning newspaper stand, he witnessed an extraordinary sight. The stand is at a busy crossroads with bus services running in all four directions.

A city gent had just bought his paper from the stand and as he turned towards the bus stop a few yards away, the driver shut the doors and pulled away.

The bus didn't get more than a few yards before it had to stop at a red light. The city gent walked to the bus door and tapped on the window, but the driver simply pointed to the next bus stop, 100 yards down the road.

As neither bus nor man could cross the road until the lights changed, the driver's suggestion inevitably meant that the man would not catch the bus.

So the gent provided his own solution; he stepped out into the road and stood immediately in front of the bus with his back to it. When the lights changed, he marched ahead of it to the next stop. The driver, unable to overtake him, had to crawl down the road to the stop, where the man got on board.

· · ·

A 68 bus in London was delayed in the rush-hour on its journey between South Croydon and Chalk Farm, because the clippie had to give a speech at every stop explaining why the lower deck was crammed full while the upstairs was empty. The heel of her shoe had broken off just before leaving the depot, and all she could find to wear as a replacement was a pair of ill-fitting slip-ons. As she was concerned about tripping on the stairs, the Duty Manager had agreed to let her keep all passengers downstairs until she could change her shoes at her home along the route.

At Crystal Palace, the passengers waited quietly for the conductress to go into her house and change her shoes. Only when she was back on board were they allowed upstairs to get a seat. A London Transport spokesman said, 'I think the conductress showed commendable initiative.'

· · ·

A housewife in Basingstoke couldn't believe her

eyes when an express train flashed by on the line at the bottom of her garden. There, doing a commendable impression of a praying mantis, was a young man sitting on the buffers.

In a panic she rang her local station and the race began to stop the 9.36 a.m. Exeter to London Waterloo. Despite emergency messages being flashed down the line, the train tore through Hook Station in Hampshire with the young man cheerily giving the passengers on the platform a regal wave. The train finally stopped for a red light, and waiting transport police moved in. The young man, completely unperturbed, jumped down from his front-row, fully air-conditioned seat to announce: 'Actually, I often travel this way.' The police insisted that the young man finish the remainder of his journey to Waterloo inside the train. In fact they handcuffed him to the guard's van just to make sure. A British Rail spokesman said they had never known a case like it, adding tersely: 'We expect our customers to travel inside our trains.'

. . .

A young man, whose leg was already in plaster after a road accident, was travelling on the London to Carlisle express. Thinking that the train was pulling into Penrith station, the man opened the door to get off. But the train was nowhere near the station and the young man was sucked out of the carriage. For ten minutes he hung on as the Lake

District sped by at 85 m.p.h. Despite mouthing for help from the passengers inside, the man was only rescued when the train finally drew into Penrith. After the event, British Rail sent the man a useful reminder letter explaining, to his surprise, that opening the doors while the train is doing 85 m.p.h. can be dangerous.

. . .

In July 1978, Sir Peter Parker, then Chairman of British Rail, set off to attend a meeting with Cumbria County Council. Due to bad traffic he arrived late at Crewe station. Waving his BR pass, Sir Peter tore through the ticket barrier and leapt onto the departing train. It was only after some time he realized that far from being on the express for Carlisle, he was in fact on the non-stopper for London.

After much cajoling he finally persuaded a guard to throw a note out of the window wrapped round a coin. The message that landed on the platform of Tamworth station, Staffordshire, read: 'Please apologize to Cumbria Council and tell them I won't be able to make it.' As soon as he arrived back in London, Sir Peter set off for the North once more, this time by plane, adding, 'It just goes to show that it can happen to anyone.'

. . .

Progress being what it is, by 1980 it was possible

to halt a high-speed passenger train with a potato. A huge King Edward was hurled from the window of an Intercity 125 as it thundered from the West Country towards London. Attached to it was a message telling signalmen to halt the service at Reading, Berkshire.

The saga began when 23 passengers told the ticket collector that they had caught the wrong train. Instead of Paddington, London, they wanted to go to Reading. An enterprising BR man requisitioned a potato from the diner, wrapped his message round it and flung it through the window just west of Bristol. The train was stopped.

· · ·

A BR passenger took positive action rather than face his wife two hours late. Realizing that another tardy arrival would cook his goose and overcook his dinner, the businessman stranded on the 5.05 p.m. from London Bridge to Eastbourne begged the driver to phone his wife to tell her he would be late home. Others, also desperate to avoid a domestic crisis, followed his example, so the driver, no doubt a married man himself, got out of his cab with a fistful of messages. Using the track-side telephone, he called a signalman who phoned the man in the control office at Redhill in Surrey who then phoned to pacify the wives.

· · ·

In 1991 a train driver took 80 passengers for a drink when a tree blocked the line, stranding them in the country. As rescue workers battled for more than an hour to clear the tracks, Richard Mayrick, 59, led his passengers to a nearby local. Buying £100 worth of drinks for the delighted commuters earned him a commendation from British Rail.

His Manchester to Cardiff train was forced to stop near Shrewsbury because gales had brought down a tree. When he was told that clearing it would take some time, Mr Mayrick said, 'I decided to take them to the pub. I checked with my local manager to see if it would be all right to give the passengers some light refreshment.'

The nearby Albion pub was having a quiet night before the commuters arrived, but landlady Mrs Joyce Chapman soon had one of her busiest.

. . .

A Colchester commuter slept through his stop, the one after that and the one after that. He woke up just as the train was joining the Hook of Holland ferry. Indeed, stories of commuters sleeping across, or nearly across, borders are not unusual. New Yorkers on their way home to Connecticut have been known to reach the Canadian border, while London commuters end up comatose in Wales with some frequency. Most oversleeping commuters are apprehended at frontiers, but two men who boarded a train at Victoria en route for Carshalton wound up in Dunkirk. They had boarded the Dover train by mistake, and only woke when the ferry was approaching the French port. Back in England 48 hours later one of them, a bus driver, said that the previous two days had been a nightmare, but he predicted that things would get worse when he tried to explain the whole escapade to his wife.

. . .

Rail passengers in Norfolk became crabby when they realized that a consignment of commuting whelks was being given preferential treatment. The 10.08 a.m. from Wells to Kings Lynn used to arrive at Dereham with a cargo of the smelly molluscs. On the other platform would be the 9.53 a.m. from Kings Lynn to Norwich. The whelks were also bound for Norwich, but to save heaving them from one train to the other, the staff at Dereham Station left them where they were and asked the passengers to move instead. Resenting having to carry luggage up and down two flights of stairs and across an open bridge, several travellers complained. As one commented gruffly, 'It's a shell of a way to go.'

. . .

Commuters on the Brighton to London line were asked to keep their coffee cup lids or go thirsty on the 70-minute trip. One traveller, film producer Robert Sidaway, was even refused service unless he signed a disclaimer saying he would not sue if his coffee spilt and burnt him.

Mr Sidaway was so insulted at this gesture that he refused to sign. A BR spokesman trying to take the heat out of the situation said: 'There is no policy of asking passengers to keep their lids. This sounds like an off-the-cuff remark.'

· · ·

To the surprise of those on board, an enormous black Labrador dog caught a District Line train somewhere near Barking and stretched out at full length to snore the journey away. The 8.30 a.m. train was at the height of the rush-hour and the dog was occupying enough space for half a dozen passengers. By the time the train approached Mile End, the passengers were approaching mutiny; 'And on a Monday morning too,' one of them snapped. But the supine dog was rather big, and the passengers remembered well that old saying about letting sleeping dogs, etc. As the train continued on its way, the dog looked more and more contented and the passengers more and more put out. At Mansion House, however, commuters acted. The Labrador stretched, yawned and allowed itself to be led away, albeit a little reluctantly. One passenger said: 'We've heard jokes about commuters being sardines in tins and cattle in trucks, now we're going to be catching the 8.30 kennel to town.'

· · ·

In New Delhi, newspapers carried a large advertisement reading 'Passengers on Western and Southern Railways are requested not to carry explosives as personal baggage with them on journeys. This practice has led to several accidents and fires in railway compartments.'

. . .

It's advisable for anyone travelling on the Red Arrow from Moscow to St Petersburg to take a pair of ear-plugs, for the midnight flyer is known as the Lovers' Express. The sexiest train in the world carries young couples with nowhere else to go, husbands cheating on their wives, and men and women who only discovered each other's attraction through the fumes of vodka a couple of hours earlier.

They all catch the train as booking into a hotel for a night of steamy passion is almost impossible; instead they opt for a night of steaming passion.

One line-lover was Alexei, a 21-year-old office worker who arrived on the platform wearing jeans, T-shirt and a huge smile. He boarded the train with his student girlfriend Elena. Alexei said, 'Every month for a year now we have been doing this. I live with my mother and Elena is in a hostel at the university. Only on the train can we spend the whole night together. We save all our money and every month we have a whole two nights in which to make love all night. It is good, yes?'

Often the couples board with no luggage at all,

or just the smallest of overnight bags. Each first-class compartment has two narrow but comfortable beds, blinds, curtains and soft lighting.

When Alexei was asked if the train's rattling and shaking put him off at all, he shook his head and said proudly, 'Me? I'm an athlete.'

· · ·

In 1992, a gang of youths boarded a Moscow commuter train and guarded the doors to prevent anyone from leaving. Then to the amazement of the trapped commuters, a couple lay down in the middle of the carriage and made love. The embarrassed commuters averted their eyes from such an explicit performance but when the couple had finished, the youths guarding the doors came round and demanded five roubles from everyone for watching the show. Pensioners, however, were given a reduction and only had to pay three roubles.

· · ·

In 1985, there was an exhibition of underground railway maps, as an esoteric art form, in a New York Subway station. As art it may have worked, but as a way of helping passengers it did not. Puzzled out-of-towners were seen frowning over underground maps from London, Paris and Moscow.

· · ·

Few people know this, but the New York Subway actually employs 'sniffers' – men who sniff out poisonous fumes or gas leaks in the city's underground railway system. The doyen of the sniffers is known as 'Smelly Kelly', who has more than thirty years' experience behind him, during which he has come to recognize almost every smell known to man. When a whiff so potent that it was making people faint suffused one station, Smelly declared it to be elephants. Elephants it had to be, and elephants it was. The station turned out to be underneath the site of a long-closed circus, and a burst water pipe had soaked buried elephant dung. Thus the fumes.

. . .

Old 'Shirts' Blanton, confined to a wheelchair in his shack by the railway track, had a surprise on Christmas Eve in 1972. The Washington to Central Florida train made an unscheduled stop by his home, so that passengers could give him an impromptu carol service.

. . .

On the Tokyo underground the sight of rows of overworked businessmen sleeping, and office ladies snoring, is so commonplace that no one took any notice of the still form of the middle-aged man in the fifth carriage. It was only five hours and two round trips of the Sobu Line later, when the train was being checked before going back to the depot, that it was discovered that the man was not in a deep sleep but in fact was dead.

Apparently not one of the scores of people who sat next to him had noticed that the man had passed away. Police said later that the cause of death was probably a heart attack shortly after the man boarded the train.

Japan has coined a new phrase for the phenomenon of death by overwork – *karoshi*. It has not yet come up for a term for death by overwork while on a train.

. . .

Sweden's Inlandsbana railway, which ran from Stockholm up to the Arctic Circle and the Midnight Sun, closed in 1991 due to lack of subsidy. But at the time the reason given for the closure was rather more imaginative. The line was just too dull.

The Swedish Transport Ministry complained that during the 1,000-km journey the only view was of fir trees, fir trees and more fir trees. With the exception of the odd lake and stray elk, the view for the two-day journey was solely of trees. Nature-lovers and fir-tree fanciers naturally cited this as the very reason why the rail line should remain open.

In its 55-year life the journey became very popular with Interrailers. In fact there were so many young travellers that conductors were issued with multilingual phrase-books containing translations of 'Look, there is an elk!' and 'Look, there is a reindeer!' The question 'Look, is that another fir tree?' was not listed in the book.

. . .

Norwegian train drivers, meanwhile, are issued with shotguns as standard snow equipment. The trouble is that moose and reindeer walk the tracks which offer a clear path through the snow. If a train hits one by accident, the driver has to get out, track it and shoot it, if it has been injured. Passengers sit and wait while the driver undertakes his mission of mercy. In Sweden, where several thousand reindeer are killed every year by trains, the railways appealed to the public for ideas on scaring roaming beasts from the lines. One idea was a new type of whistle several tones lower than usual and which sounded like the roaring of a lion – but tests left the reindeer unmoved.

Special detonators were also tried, but failed to impress the reindeer let alone intimidate them. A herd of some 30 animals barely noticed the detonations, and failed to budge. Seconds later they were nosing round the smoking remains to see if they were edible.

. . .

Eighteen funeral urns, complete with contents, were among the 1,812,229 items of lost property on Japanese national railways in 1978. There were also 114 sets of false teeth, assorted rabbits and chickens, 470,000 umbrellas and a large amount of money. Only about a third of the goods accidentally left on the trains were reclaimed, while all but a pocketful of the £500,000 cash found a claimant.

6

Kafka Commutes

BUSES THAT ARE officially trains, stations that officially don't exist but are used every day, fare structures that would have Alice booted out of Wonderland . . . the spirit of Franz Kafka lives on in the commuting funny farms of the late twentieth century. Why transport should attract such loopiness all over the world is not entirely clear. Perhaps, like the best lunatics, officials (and occasionally barmy passengers) don't realize they are being irrational. Or maybe they are simply out to amuse us? Either way, we hope that they never give up or become disappointingly coherent. Life wouldn't be the same, somehow, without baffled commuters, red-faced officials and embarrassed spokesmen.

. . .

An art historian, Tim Barranger, was taking his new wife to Leeds. When he boarded the train at Ilkley he explained to the inspector on board that he wanted the cheapest day-return. He and his wife were going shopping and would be back at about 6 p.m. The inspector duly issued a ticket, but when Mr Barranger tried to get off at Leeds the same inspector barred him from doing so. His explanation – almost as surreal as what was happening –

was that on the cheapest ticket Mr Barranger could travel there and back, but regrettably not get off in between. On hearing this absurd logic, the other passengers marched the offending inspector to the station master's office. 'Oh Bernard,' said the station master, slumping at his desk in despair, 'not again. What have you done now?'

.   .   .

British Rail once introduced a new special service on the Birmingham to Lichfield line, distinctive because the trains were to run empty. The section of line BR chose for this revolutionary system was one on which they had always refused to run trains before, because it would be uneconomic. The trains were to carry passengers to a new commuter station at Blake Street, half-way down the line. Then they would head off to Lichfield seven miles away to turn round and come back again. Signals were eventually going to be installed that would let the trains turn round at Blake Street, but in the meantime, as a BR spokesman prudently put it, 'We do not intend to allow passengers on these extra trains on the trip to Lichfield to see if that would generate extra business. We do not want the hassle when they are withdrawn after the signals are put in.'

.   .   .

In 1958, the government of Bombay considered

sanctioning special rates for road mileage for government servants travelling on camels.

The government decided that the rates for servants in the first and second grades were quite adequate, but those for the third and fourth grades were unacceptable. They agreed the following special rates: 'A government servant of the third grade: the actual cost of hiring a camel limited to 8*d* per mile. A servant of the fourth grade: the actual cost of hiring a camel limited to $4\frac{3}{4}d$ per mile.'

As if this were not sufficient, every travel allowance bill, in which road mileage at the rates mentioned was claimed, had to include a recorded certificate to the effect that the government servant concerned had actually travelled by camel. The government said this was only a precaution in the public interest, although the directive gave no clue as to the baffling question of why a government servant might want to commute by camel unless it were strictly necessary.

. . .

Police saw a woman walking her dog along the hard shoulder of the M25. When asked exactly what she was doing, she replied nonchalantly, 'I'm heading for the M11.'

. . .

In 1991, a national newspaper ran a story which stated that the M25 would run clockwise and anticlockwise on alternate days. This idea intrigued one Cabinet minister who asked Malcolm Rifkind, then Transport Secretary, 'How's your M25 plan coming along?' Mr Rifkind had to point out with great diplomacy that the date on which the story had been published was April the First.

. . .

A Norwich travel company organized an M25 sightseeing trip, advertised as 'a complete circuit of the London Orbital Motorway', with a chance to 'listen to an interesting and informative commentary by our courier'.

Eighteen people paid £8.90 each to travel anticlockwise around it, with a courier on hand to point out the landmarks and special features of the 117-mile journey. One tripper explained excitedly that he was already acquainted with parts of the M25: 'When we went to Boulogne we saw a bit from the M11 to the Dartford Tunnel, then when we went to Heathrow we saw the section to South Mimms. But the rest of it is completely new to us.'

. . .

When Barry Black was named Commuter of the Year, he was sacked by his construction company. The day after receiving the title from Radio 2 DJ Tony Brandon, Barry was asked to leave because the firm was unhappy about the publicity. They might have been seen as doing him a favour; Barry was making a 342-mile round trip every day from Gwent, South Wales, to London. He got up at 5.30 a.m. in the morning and spent over £1,000 on train fares per year. But the hero commuter immediately took on another job in the same area, so his commut-a-thon continued. Barry's prize was a three-day family holiday with British Rail.

. . .

In February 1991, a British Rail spokesman became famous, even though anonymous, when he explained that trains had been halted by a form of fine snow that made the wheels slip. The spokesman probably thought no more about it, until the newspapers, as they do, put his explanation in a subtly different light. 'The wrong kind of snow' became an un-slogan for BR, and captivated the public, although no BR person had ever in fact said it. Since then 'leaves on the line', an excuse relying on the unfortunate (and evidently brand-new) tendency of trees to shed their leaves in autumn, has joined The Wrong Kind Of Snow as a national catchphrase. Now, passengers in Wiltshire have discovered there is a 'wrong type of rain' – a fine drizzle known only to BR officials which causes a pulp on the tracks and makes the wheels spin. But BR were as confused as the passengers at Paddington station when they were told that services would be disrupted by 'a train on the track', which everybody thought was precisely the kind of thing you need to sustain a service. Another station announcer at Paddington found himself saying, 'We have lost your train.' The driver, it turned out, could not find his train in the fog. Only when the fog cleared enough for him to find it parked in a siding could the commuters go home. On another notable occasion, passengers were told about 'llamas on the line'. The beasts, stubbornly grazing between Didcot and Reading, had escaped from a nearby zoo.

. . .

In 1983, tired travellers being rescued from a stranded train found themselves lost down a pitch-black country lane. The driver of the bus taking the 20 passengers on a 15-minute journey from one station to another had got confused by the unfamiliar roads and bridges. To make matters worse the BR 'guide' accompanying them, who had dozed off, suddenly woke up and started a slanging match with the bus driver that only ended when a passenger in a pinstripe suit who also knew the route intervened. With the commuter crisply barking out route instructions, the 20 passengers finally reached their train.

. . .

Passengers on a 1.15 p.m. train from King's Cross to Leeds were handed a foolscap questionnaire asking them what they considered to be most important on a railway – punctuality, speed or comfort. As the forms were being collected, the train was delayed at Peterborough, due to an axle overheating. Then, near Grantham, there was a wait of 40 minutes while a broken-down diesel engine was removed from the track. Finally the lights failed and the train arrived in almost complete darkness more than an hour late, resounding to the mutinous clamour of passengers demanding their forms back.

. . .

In August 1991, the journalist Joanna Coles told *Spectator* readers about her outlandish Intercity journey from Edinburgh to London. Twenty minutes into the journey, she was approached by the conductor and asked to move. When Joanna refused on the grounds that she had both paid for and reserved the seat, the conductor went berserk and demanded her home address, which she refused to give. So the conductor went to call the police, who boarded the train at the next stop. The two officers refused to accept Joanna's business card as a legal address and asked her to leave the train at Newcastle where they could charge her for obstructing their enquiries. After ten minutes of arguing, Joanna finally gave in. To add insult to injury, the train arrived at King's Cross over two hours late. As a result of the article, Joanna received over 100 letters of support, with people pledging to write to the Ministry of Transport and British Rail on her behalf. No sooner had the *Spectator* hit the newsstands than Joanna was contacted by a constable from the Police Complaints Authority. The constable said that he was appalled by what had happened and assured Joanna that two officers would be down from York the following week.

British Rail, however, were a little slower to react to the article. When the *Sunday Telegraph* (who had also run Joanna's story) contacted BR on Joanna's behalf, they were informed that if she lodged an 'official complaint' the matter would be investigated. Joanna wrote to Sir Bob Reid, the BR Chairman, who replied by return of post, offering her a free first-class ticket and reassuring her that the 'appropriate action would be taken with the staff concerned'. When she wrote again three months later, to enquire as to the 'result' of this action, she was assured by Sir Bob that a Mr Baptie had been 'counselled' by his manager.

. . .

At Liverpool Street station passengers are baffled when they go searching for platform 19. There it is, advertised up on the announcement screen, but get past platform 18 and there is nothing more. Mrs Somerset Ogden found this out when she was going to meet a friend. 'I was waiting at platform 6 when an announcement came up that the train would be coming into platform 19. So I picked up my two-year-old son and the trolley, and went in search of the platform. When I couldn't find it, I asked a porter who informed me that it didn't exist.' More than a little confused, Mrs Ogden checked the board again and then went to the manager's office, and marched him out to look at the information. Sighing, he explained that – as must surely be obvious – when a platform was not allocated to a train, the computer automatically printed up platform 19, on the grounds that there was no platform 19. Mrs Ogden finally met her friend on the altogether more prosaic platform 10.

. . .

British Rail also has entire trains that don't exist. In an attempt to make rush-hour trains arrive on time, BR went to the length of convincing passengers that trains they thought they could see were, in fact, a mirage. Route managers came to the conclusion that Intercity's time was being wasted by passengers boarding when they should have been using a local service. So BR's message to passengers was that although the train looked real enough, was advertised as going to the station they required and was only half full, it didn't really exist. Experts worked out that it takes only one minute for a passenger to disembark from a train, but a whole three minutes to get on board, and this two-minute difference was causing all the trouble. BR then went on to admit that the train would, in all probability, be late whether passengers got on it or not, but insisted this was not the point. To help passengers comply with the rule, BR introduced a deterrent. Anyone boarding an Intercity would have to pay the fare from the last stop; if the train had been going non-stop since Newcastle or Manchester, it could turn out to be a very expensive journey.

. . .

In 1988, a train that had been axed by Dr Beeching 22 years earlier finally stopped. The service, which had not been timetabled since 1964, ran every morning at dawn to take workers to a Rolls-Royce factory, dropping them off at a station called Filton North, in Bristol, which was not even marked on modern maps.

Every afternoon at precisely 4.14 p.m., the train that didn't exist waited at the station that also didn't exist to take the workers home – a three-minute trip. A BR spokesman commented: 'As far as we are concerned this train doesn't exist.' He added for clarity, 'Filton North station was closed in 1964.'

. . .

The end of the holiday season means a return to *tsukin-jigoku* or commuter hell for thousands of Japanese businessmen. In order to avoid it, some commuters speed into the centre of the city by car in the small hours of the morning. Parking in front of the city gardens, they sleep for a while and eat a boxed breakfast brought from home, before starting out for the day's work.

A New Jersey attorney explained in unequivocal terms why the state would not increase commuter railroad subsidies: 'It would be cheaper to buy each passenger a Volkswagen and send him off to work.'

.   .   .

Signor Bettino del Priore finally got the job he had always wanted – station master for the world's smallest state railway.

The one-hour-a-day job entailed looking after a double-line track in the Vatican City. It wasn't a particularly taxing position because the track ran for only 400 yards and finished in a cul-de-sac tunnel.

The trains were not very frequent either, although the occasional one would bring news-papers, petrol and cement to the Vatican.

.   .   .

An express train was stopped at Brescia in Northern Italy by two garrulous housewives. The two women were so intent on their mid-track gossip that they didn't hear the oncoming train nor even its urgent whistle. When the driver invited them to leave the line, they stepped aside unconcernedly and carried on chatting.

.   .   .

Minnie Parker, an 83-year-old widow, was that rare bird, a voluntary commuter. Getting up at 5.30 a.m., she would leave her home in Leeds to begin her journey on a milk float. The milkman gave her a lift to Leeds bus station in time to catch the number 44 at 7.45 a.m. Three hours later, she would have an early lunch in Bridlington. After a walk on the seafront, she would get the 4.30 p.m. bus back to Leeds. There she caught a municipal bus home and went to bed at 9 p.m. The reason for this daily trek is simple: 'Because I love the journey – and the Bridlington air.'

.   .   .

In 1976, it was reported that on the Hanley to Bagnall route in Staffordshire the buses no longer stopped for passengers. This quirky aberration was noticed by Mr Bill Hancock who complained about the buses' penchant for whizzing past crowds of waiting passengers. Councillor Arthur Cholerton was then called in to investigate the problem. He pointed out quite reasonably that if buses continually stopped to pick up people, their timetables might be messed up.

.   .   .

A safety-conscious commuter received due thanks for his concern about overcrowding on the Tube – he was arrested. Mr Christopher Sutton, a television producer from Finsbury Park, approached an official at Oxford Circus station to tell him of a bottleneck that was causing danger to commuters. As Mr Sutton had reached the top of the escalators, he nearly tripped over a mass of bodies, almost prostrate because they were being shoved forward. The problem had been caused by the fact that only two ticket barriers were open.

Mr Sutton, trying to make Tube staff aware of this problem, was told to address his complaints to 55 The Broadway (London Transport Headquarters). Incredulous that such a matter was dismissed so lightly, Mr Sutton became annoyed and insisted that something was done. At this point transport police arrested him and dragged him into a nearby office. Mr Constantine Fernando, who owns a sweet-shop in the booking hall, described what happened: 'They literally dragged him into the room. He was shouting "Help me, help me". So I walked into the room and told him not to worry, I'd take the names and addresses of the people who had witnessed it.' The magistrate in charge of Mr Sutton's case, however, saw that justice was finally set back on the rails. Dismissing the accusations, she congratulated him, observing, 'I find it a great relief that people like you are still around.'

. . .

Donald Gordon, the former president of the Canadian railways, told a government inquiry that the reason he carried a small screwdriver in his pocket when he travelled on trains was to tighten up loose pieces of equipment in order to stop squeaks. 'With a little ingenuity you can make a lot of improvements,' he said.

.   .   .

Ralph Ranson held the record as British Rail's longest-serving commuter for his 73 years of to-ing and fro-ing. Having travelled almost every day for most of his life, Ralph had clocked up enough miles to equal going round the world 10 times. His record aside, the most unusual thing about him was that he wouldn't hear a bad word said about BR. 'The trains I use are perfect for time,' he said. 'When my wife hears the train arrive at 6.20 she knows she can expect me home 12–15 minutes later. There is no other form of transport that gives you that kind of service.' Staff at Cannon Street were just as complimentary about Ralph. According to railwayman Bob Marsh, 'He was the ideal commuter, you could set your watch by him.' Mr Ranson's record was later overtaken when a Mr Ratcliff-Steel retired after hitting his eighty-third year. He was still buying the same ticket from Bexley to London. BR put on an elaborate reception for him at Victoria. His gracious response: 'All this carry-on has made me late for work today. Still, it's only once in a lifetime.'

.   .   .

Oldham Athletic Football Club protested to British Rail because a train left on time. As players and officials arrived at Euston station after playing Chelsea, they were amazed to see their soccer special pulling out of the station. Oldham secretary, Tom Finn, said, 'We shall be asking for some form of compensation. I have never known a special train set off exactly on time.'

.　.　.

Two young boys were waiting patiently one Sunday at the railway station hoping to catch the train into town to see the latest film. As the train approached the tiny station at Hamble near Southampton, the 14-year-olds, David Lashbrook and John Henderson, prepared to get on board. But instead the driver leant out and called to them 'We only stopped here to tell you that we don't stop here on Sundays.' With that he and his train disappeared in a cloud of diesel fumes.

The two boys had to walk half a mile down the track to Netley where the trains did actually stop on Sundays. A BR spokesman agreed that the guard had been a little 'over-zealous'. 'His common sense should have told him that he might have allowed the passengers to get on the train once it has stopped.'

.　.　.

The Soviet paper *Literaturnaya Gazeta*, inundated with letters of complaint about the railways, decided to investigate for themselves. When a journalist from the paper asked an official at the ministry of railways for his definition of an express train, the official accused him of interfering and referred him to the chief engineer. Unfortunately the chief engineer didn't have an explanation either and the hapless journalist was passed on to another department.

Finally the reporter bumped into the minister himself who said he would be delighted to answer any questions put to him. So the questions were written out and sent to the ministry. After waiting five months with no reply, the paper rang the ministry, confirmed that the questions had actually been delivered, and then published the interview with no answers. It ran something like this: *Q:* If I am not mistaken, trains in our country carry 3,500 million people a year? *Answer* . . . *Q:* Are readers right in saying that last summer the trains still did not run on time? *Answer* . . . *Q:* Can you explain why passenger trains, without increasing their speed, suddenly became expresses? *Answer* . . . The questions steadily became more embarrassing, but still no answers. Finally one ministry official stuck his neck out and gave an answer. He said an express was called an express not because it went faster but because it afforded greater comfort. The passengers should have guessed.

. . .

It was discovered in 1983 that large sections of the

Soviet railways were falling to pieces because repair workers were selling the wooden sleepers on the black market. As a result, thousands of trains ran late each year. An investigation showed that 190,000 sleepers had been sold illegally that year in the Moscow region alone. In the same year, there was a record increase in commuter vandalism. Passengers were urged to stop hooligans from smashing up carriages. A total of 2,720 loudspeakers were also stolen from the trains by people described with soothing bureaucratic euphemism as 'radio fans'.

. . .

Another Russian dissatisfied with the state of the railways was *Krokodil*, the only pre-*glasnost* publication that was permitted to be ironic about the life in the USSR. One *Krokodil* reporter took it upon himself to highlight the chaos at Kharkov station, the Crewe Junction of the Soviet Union. This investigator described the scene at Kharkov as follows: 'The loudspeaker announced – to everyone's astonishment – that train number 78 from Kiev was due at platform 3. A crowd of people rushed there carrying big bouquets. But to no one's great amazement, no train ever came. It transpired that the station staff had received the wrong instructions. In the midst of the mayhem the loudspeaker made another announcement – not about approaching trains, but instead suggesting that comrades might come to see a new film in the waiting room entitled *Girl Keeps a Date*. Other passengers were offered alternative ways of killing time – personally conducted tours of the city parks, or talks on interplanetary travel. While the passengers were spoilt for choice in some respects, it seemed that actually getting a ticket was another matter altogether.

An elderly traveller with a big, heavy suitcase approached an official in a red cap and asked how to get to Jevpatoria. The official told him that the next train was the following day – and suggested the gentleman *might* use the time by catching up with *Girl Keeps a Date*.

. . .

The Begum of Oudh, a stately 52-year-old Muslim aristocrat, had been living with her son, daughter, servants and dogs in the VIP buildings of the New Delhi railway station for 12 years. And for almost as long, the station master had been trying to evict her. The Begum's hand-made, gold-embossed writing paper stated her title – HRH the Begum of Oudh, Shehzadi Wilayat Mahal, heir to the last king of Oudh – and gave her address as 'The Rulers in Exile, New Delhi Railway Station'.

The two-storey red-and-cream building, intended to receive prime ministers and presidents, stands back from platform 1. The Begum had barricaded the approaches in discreet good taste with a fence of plant pots. Trespassers were kept at bay by a pair of snarling Dobermans. The station master kept his distance but pressed the government to evict the family, who moved in after their last remaining palace in Lucknow was burned to the ground in 1971.

After much wrangling the family was offered a modern house in Lucknow, but the Begum rejected it with scorn. 'Can you imagine a Queen living in a bungalow?' she said. 'It's not good enough even for my dogs. I'd prefer to die here than accept dishonour.'

. . .

The chairman of the Indian railway board began a sit-in on one of his own trains after the railways ministry had refused him permission to travel on the board's business.

Mr B. C. Ganguli boarded a special air-conditioned saloon carriage on the Chetak express from New Delhi to Ahmadabad from where he was to begin a nine-day inspection tour of Gujarat. He was accompanied by his family and board officials. About one and a half miles out of the station, the train was stopped on the orders of Mr Hanumananthaiya, the railway minister. The railway chairman's special carriage was then detached and the rest of the train went on without him. Still sitting in his coach, Mr Ganguli said, 'This is the biggest insult ever meted out to the highest executive of the railway. I will not leave this carriage until I know the reasons for the action.'

The reason for the action was not forthcoming, so Mr Ganguli sat there with his family for six days. When asked by journalists whether he thought the row would be sorted out, the by now unshaven Mr Ganguli replied enigmatically, 'Quo Vadis?'

While he made his protest, Mrs Gandhi, the Indian Prime Minister, called the Cabinet together for an emergency meeting to resolve the long-standing squabble between the two men. Mr Hanumananthaiya said in defence of his actions that Mr Ganguli had been ordered by the ministry to cancel his tour but had refused, and therefore preventive action had become necessary.

Mr Ganguli finally returned home to Delhi six days after being prematurely retired by Mrs Gandhi. The whole affair is said to have amused the Indian public. One onlooker was Mrs Imelda Marcos – who was visiting the country to study, among other things, the technical know-how of the Indian railway system.

. . .

Francisco Marino, a 30-year-old Mexican dishwasher, lost an arm when he fell on the track in the New York Subway and was hit by a train. He was at the time in a state of severe inebriation. A Bronx jury, however, awarded him $9.3 million after finding that the Transit Authority had negligently failed to protect him.

Mr Marino's objection was that the man at the

token booth had noticed how drunk he was but had failed to obey a ruling requiring staff to have intoxicated people removed from the station. Mr Marino's lawyers successfully argued that the accident deprived him of his dishwashing abilities and the huge pay-out covered his pain, anguish, and loss of earnings.

On hearing the result, outraged officials of New York's Transit Authority immediately launched an appeal. Mr Marino, meanwhile, turned understandably patriotic and exclaimed 'God Bless America'.

If you must have a commuting mishap, there is no question that New York is the place for it. A Brooklyn jury later awarded $31 million to another arguably lucky accident victim, whose legs were severed when he fell from the platform and was struck by a train. The jury felt that the driver was negligent in failing to stop the train in time. Even a man who jumped deliberately in front of a train, and survived, was awarded $600,000. Within days of this, the city authorities reported a dramatic jump in 'accidents' on the Subway and bus system.

. . .

Nowhere is Germany's love of rules more evident than in the section of the country's railway traffic regulations on carrying corpses. Four out of 96 of these regulations relate to the dead. Each corpse must have the proper documents. Since every

German has to have an identity card, a dead person travelling through Germany courtesy of the train must have a passport. Section 44, paragraph 4, rules that this document has to be handed over to the recipient of the corpse. The sender is not allowed to use express trains for his cargo, though he must fill in an express waybill. Paragraph 5 states that 'Corpses must not be sent cash-on-delivery', and the railway threatens that anyone sending corpses under false cover is liable to be charged four times the normal rate. There is even a special ruling for corpses destined for the dissection room. They can be transported unattended but no food or semi-luxury can be added to the consignment.

. . .

The United States has a highly complex but ingenious way of realigning train timetables on the night the clocks go back. All across the USA regardless of location, trains simply stop at 2 a.m. and then start off again an hour later. Some 45 overnight trains and 7,000 passenger trains come to a halt, often in the middle of nowhere, and the passengers are stranded until it is officially 2 a.m. again and the timetables have caught up.

In spring the same complex system is put into motion once again, but this time the trains go faster to catch up. There may be less disruptive ways of solving the problem, but Mr Claytor, the President of Amtrak, doesn't think so. He suggests that passengers look for the positive side of being in limbo for an hour, saying: 'Don't miss this once-a-year opportunity to sleep an extra hour on Amtrak.'

. . .

Penn Central, a conglomeration of sections of the US railroad system, was accused of running down passenger services with the aim of forcing a government takeover. The company rejected such allegations despite the full-page advert it had just run in the *New York Times* reading, 'You say our service is bad. We agree.'

. . .

Penn Central's monthly report used to boast a 92.4 per cent punctuality record until an investigator from the state controller's office paid them a visit. He arrived on the train 15 minutes late, only to be told that he was in fact on time.

A check was then carried out on the 500 trains running in and out of the New York station daily. When the results were compared with the records there was a 53 per cent error. The findings reinforced the belief of 67,000 commuters that their watches were not actually wrong on a daily basis.

One dispatch clerk called upon to explain the book-cooking said: 'By making these small adjustments, I minimized the explanation workload. It was bad enough having the trains run late, but explaining that in detail just meant more work for everyone, and the books looked awful.'

. . .

During a guards' strike, a beleaguered Waterloo ticket collector told reporters of the abuse he and his colleagues took from frustrated commuters. A guard on go-slow was understanding but added: 'We're all in the same boat. Most of us have got to come to work by train too.'

7

Future Perfect

THERE IS AN odd contradiction right across the commuting world; while all transport systems do their best to make life unpleasant for the commuter, they insist at the same time on testing improvements and innovations to their services, ostensibly for the commuter's good. We believe after careful study that all such breakthroughs are in fact part of an elaborate hoax, an international competition among transport authorities to come up with the stupidest 'improvement'. Although commuting innovations are always trumpeted in the local newspapers, they are rarely reported when the gimmicks inevitably fail and are shunted into a quiet siding.

. . .

In October 1991, the inhumane conditions on Japan's rush-hour trains led the East Japan Railway Company to add an extra carriage to every train on its Tokyo loop-line. This carriage, however, was to be different from the rest. During peak times there would be no seats, only standing room. But at 10 a.m., when most of the rush was over, collapsible chairs flipped down from lockers, as if appearing from nowhere.

. . .

Italian state railways once announced that the Rome–Milan express would have experimental private radios for passengers. The radios, concealed in the head cushions, would be inaudible unless the head actually rested against the cushion. The radio offered three channels – one with music, one with news, sport, commentary and dramatic pieces, and the third was a multilingual commentary on the countryside interspersed with station announcements.

. . .

In 1991, East Japan Railways devised a bleeper box to prevent passengers from overriding their destinations.

The device can recognize the different high-frequency waves from radio transmitters beside various stations. The device will recognize which particular station the train is approaching from its radio signal and thus warn the passenger with a series of electronic sounds.

The prototype model is the size of a credit card and equipped with earphone and built-in microphone. JR East plan to add a radio, calculator and clock functions. 'The device works well in packed trains and even in the toilets,' said a spokesman.

. . .

East Japan Railways have installed new sensors

under their carriages to gauge how full the carriages are, so that stations further down the line can be advised.

The old method of railway employees estimating the capacity of a carriage by looking through the windows proved to be too unreliable.

The new devices are connected to the air springs installed under the carriages to absorb shocks. The number of passengers is calculated on the assumption that each passenger weighs 60 kg. This information allows passengers at stations further up the line to be directed into the less crowded compartments.

. . .

Ever felt tense on the Tube? Experts suggest that a whiff of the seaside or a blast of country air piped into the Underground would calm stressed passengers and ease rush-hour mania. The smells that work best are those which remind the passenger of holidays and fresh air, according to researchers from Warwick University, part of whose work was sponsored by the perfume trade. London Transport declined to comment on the 'Happy Odour' plan, saying it was unaware of the research team's proposals.

. . .

Professor Tom Singleton and his team from the psychology department at Aston University attached electrodes to the heads of business executives and top civil servants as they studied the contents of their briefcases on trains from the Midlands to London. 'We're trying to discover if rail journeys have any effect on these people in their decision-making,' the professor explained. He did not elaborate on whether a parallel study might look at the effects of electrodes being taped to the head while making decisions on a train.

.   .   .

British Rail officials at Birmingham's New Street station decided to change the piped music played on the station concourse from the usual nerve-soothing muzak to military band numbers in an attempt to get passengers to clear the station more quickly. The *Daily Mail* reported that the 11,000 rush-hour commuters marched out in brisk step with 'Colonel Bogey' and 'The Yellow Rose of Texas'.

.   .   .

In 1991, German passengers finally got what they wanted after a decade of waiting – a supertrain. The first streamlined bullet-shaped express was launched, but its inaugural run was more of an inaugural limp. In Munich, there was a brass band reception to welcome the new service with free beer for everyone. Unfortunately a party of visitors on board one of the supertrains were shunted into an automatic train-washing shed by mistake. Then there was a spate of breakdowns, from the engines to the super-flush lavatories to the microwaves to the beer cooler in the restaurant. Half the new trains were up to 50 minutes late on their first day, disrupting normal services and delaying thousands of commuters. The result was that although 90 per cent of the first-class tickets had been pre-sold for the following three weeks, all 25 trains had to be taken out of service and overhauled.

. . .

Car enthusiast David Mattla came up with an idea to combat the stress generated during traffic jams – dashboard pin-ups and taped messages from a lover. Mr Mattla said, 'The irate motorist can switch on a tape of his wife or girlfriend. Whispered sweet nothings or photographs can prevent headaches and pile-ups.' Oh yeah.

. . .

The Romans were better at commuting innovations than any modern society. Surviving surfaces of Roman roads give clear indications that the normal gauge of Roman carts was about 4 feet 8 inches. This measurement is remarkable when you remember that the gauge of modern railways, constructed 1,800 years later, is exactly the same – as is the axle-width of modern cars.

Ancient Roman commuting could also be quicker than the misery British commuters suffer today. In Roman Britain a normal day's journey for an official worked out at 50 miles. In emergency, horse relays were used for maximum speed. It is known that the Emperor Tiberius covered 200 miles in 24 hours in this manner. Two thousand years later, a survey by the Department of Transport predicted that without major improvements to the road network, the average speed of a car in central London would be as little as 5 m.p.h. by the turn of the century.

. . .

Nigerians began to realize how hopeless most modern transport innovations were when a monorail was mooted in an attempt to ease congestion in Lagos.

Other alternatives had failed. An attempt to restrict the number of cars with a system of odd- and even-day number plates did not halve but in fact doubled the amount of traffic – people simply bought two cars, one with an odd number, the other with an even. The authorities then built a network of motorways, but instead of making for swifter journeys the four-lane roads only encouraged traffic jams four times as big.

The Lagos monorail was intended to carry 1,050,000 commuters an hour, but was shelved when the authorities realized that the city's population was growing faster than any transport system intended to carry it.

. . .

In an attempt to shame bad drivers into taking more care, driving instructor John Jackson suggested that instead of simply being banned, bad drivers should be given a 'P' plate.

The 'P' would stand for 'poor' and would sit on the bonnet as a badge of shame. The plate would be bright yellow and the driver would have to display it for a specific length of time, until, sufficiently shamed, his driving improved. (Unless, of course, the offending driver told everyone that 'P' stood for Perfect.)

. . .

A police road-safety expert from Yorkshire warned that car-owners could be driven to madness simply by the name of their vehicle. Sergeant Ken Barrell wanted car manufacturers to 'think cool' when naming their new models, because in a study of accidents the majority of cars involved had macho names.

Sergeant Barrell's black-list of cars included Thunderbird, Avenger, Interceptor and Spitfire. An aggressive name induced aggressive driving, he said, though he did not suggest why Capri drivers, who might be expected to be indolent, relaxed characters, were so arrogant on the road.

A spokesman for the Society of Manufacturers and Traders said that the idea was 'nonsensical', adding 'You might as well say that a woman behind the wheel of a Princess always drives gracefully.'

. . .

In Chicago, a car park has come up with a revolutionary new idea to stop drivers spending hours looking for their cars. Each level of the multistorey park has signs with the name of a major city, and an intercom plays music associated with that city. On one level there are signs for Paris and the gentle strains of Pearl Bailey singing 'April In Paris'.

. . .

Taxi drivers in Paris came up with a novel way of making sure that their passengers were quiet and orderly. After a spate of assaults against them, the drivers installed 'hot seats'. By simply pushing a pedal and pulling two knobs, the driver could send an electric shock to jolt the unruly passenger in the back. Although the device didn't harm the victim it certainly made them quieten down.

. . .

A level-crossing keeper at Ramsgate came up with a novel idea to keep commuters happy. Mr Arthur Cox suggested the introduction of rail hostesses, to be called Bunny Girls, on mainline trains. 'The mere presence of Bunnies would keep commuters in a benevolent state of mind,' asserted Mr Cox. A British Rail spokesman seemed a little less enthusiastic about the suggestion but assured Mr Cox that his Bunny idea would 'receive consideration'.

. . .

In 1988 (after some consideration) British Rail introduced their own version of Mr Cox's idea – enter not Bunnies but CATS (Customer Action Teams). These smiling girls board trains which are delayed for over an hour to calm angry passengers and smooth ruffled brows. Armed with mobile phones, they allow commuters to phone home, book a taxi or hotel room, and they give out free coffee to help make the waiting easier. The teams are made up of BR staff who have volunteered to be on call day or night. If a train is stranded in a remote area, they will trudge across fields to get to the passengers. Joanne Laurie, 23, from Carlisle, who was a member of the feline squad, said: 'I can be sent up to Inverness or down to Crewe. We can have three delayed trains a day or none for three weeks.' CATS denied that BR have given up trying to make trains run on time and are now simply investing in damage limitation.

. . .

A TV comedy script-writer got the brush-off from

British Rail for trying to cheer up passengers. M
Tony Edwards, who had produced scripts for th
BBC, sent samples of his work to BR saying tha
passengers got so much bad news over the tannoy
that they might appreciate a little light entertain
ment at the station. According to Mr Edwards, th
passengers, thus cheered, might accept the difficul
ties of travel more readily. BR thought the pla
was 'insulting' to passengers and refused Mr Ed
wards' offer, continuing with their own brand o
humour – announcing the departure of the 8.1
from platform 3 and then sending it out from
platform 5 half empty.

. . .

An oil company trying to improve its public imag
spent £3 million on an advertising campaign t
find 'an idea ahead of its time' that would revolu
tionize American public transport.

Not everyone was taken in by Atlantic
Richfield's 'token gesture', however, and many o
the entries – ranging from the pornographic to th
ridiculous – reflected this cynicism. They include
a giant see-saw on which passengers seated on on
end are transported by a 10-ton weight dropped o
the other, and a vast football-shaped Zeppelin tha
seats 200 people and is propelled by a giant boo
Perhaps the person who was least convinced b
the company's sincerity was the gentleman from
Los Angeles who proposed if the company wa
really serious, it should scrap the ads and donate 1

per cent of its profits to public transport research. Atlantic-Richfield said that it was just a silly mistake to have replied to him with a routine letter congratulating him on an idea ahead of its time.

.   .   .

A study of seating patterns on the Washington Metro revealed that three-quarters of adult passengers prefer to face forwards on trains but that two-thirds of children choose to face backwards. After analysing this phenomenon, experts concluded that it meant absolutely nothing. Except, of course, as one newspaper columnist sagely pointed out, that if you wait long enough in Washington, someone, somewhere will study almost anything and someone else will almost certainly print it.

.   .   .

A similar study in Leeds looked into the compelling mystery of why seats on the left-hand side of the bus always filled first.

The solution was simply that there is more to see on the left-hand side. Being seated on the left gives a perfect observation post from which to look at those getting on or off. There is also a better view of those on the pavement, of shops and gardens, and through the upstairs windows of houses.

Before this conclusion was reached, many of the public had offered their own suggestions. One said the left was preferred because there was more leg room on that side. Another claimed the reason was that it is easier to hand over the fare with your right hand if you are not left-handed.

But Mr Arnold Stone of Leeds City Transport made all the musings redundant with the real reason – straightforward nosiness.

. . .

The buses in Austin, Texas, were free to users for the year 1989–90. This innovation increased bus use by 85 per cent and won overwhelming public support. So in October 1990 the scheme was stopped. The authorities said with shimmering logic that the aim was to increase bus usership. And they had done just that.

. . .

There was great consternation in Milan when transport authorities proposed to introduce a musical strap for Milanese straphangers. The attraction of the strap was that each one played a different tune when anyone hung upon it. Or the same tune but at a different tempo. Commercial plugs by sponsors were also thrown in for good measure.

. . .

On one occasion, so many outsize passengers were crammed into the first carriage of the 7.13 a.m.

from Reading that it sank. Three times during its rush-hour journey to Paddington, the train creaked and crunched to a stop. The surprised driver found that the carriage was riding so low that a trip mechanism had hit the track and automatically applied the brakes. The only other time this happens is at a red light. A BR spokesman said that passengers would just have to spread their weight out more in future.

. . .

An inquiry into why mainline trains were so often late in Lagos came up with an unusual solution – drivers were instructed to cease their tradition of stopping the train every time they wanted to do some shopping. Apparently train drivers in Nigeria's North Central State used to halt the train when they spotted a bargain at trackside market stalls.

. . .

French railway computers were given elocution lessons in 1985, so that they could announce arrivals and departures in regional accents. The computer-controlled synthesized voices, which included a touch of Flemish for the north, a note of Provencal for the south, and something a dash more Teutonic for the east, were employed to be more reassuring for travellers.

. . .

The National Union of Railwaymen in Britain advised Japanese rail union leaders on their one area of expertise – how to wage an all-out stoppage in support of the constitutional right to strike. A team of trade union lawyers from Tokyo arrived in London in the 1970s to study British union methods of organizing industrial action.

The instruction must have been successful, for the growing phenomenon of striking in Japan was named *Eikoku byo*, which translates as the English disease.

. . .

For a select and lucky few commuters in Stockholm, work starts the minute they set foot on the train in the morning. ASEA, a nuclear and electrical multinational, has specially converted a train into offices so that their employees can use the two-hour journey as part of the working day. The train was adapted at the cost of £400,000 and is equipped with desks, computers and dial-anywhere phones. This mobile office is run by four girls who operate the switchboard, clean the desks and fitted carpets, and make tea and coffee.

. . .

In order to meet Germany's strict anti-pollution laws, in 1992 catering companies who supply food in the railways came up with the ultimate answer: edible plates made of bread and maize.

A West German railway official unearthed secret plans by Hitler to build a transcontinental railway with engines and carriages the size of houses. The double-decker trains were to have been 22 ft 5 in high and 19 ft 8 in wide, running on tracks with a gauge of 9 ft 10 in. The trains were to have run at speeds of 155 m.p.h. from the River Volga to Paris, and from Hamburg to Istanbul. The carriages would have been fitted out in the style of a luxury transatlantic liner. First-class passengers were to have carpeted reception rooms, armchairs, dressing tables and showers. The sleeping compartments were to be panelled with polished wood, dark for the gentlemen and light for the ladies. East Europeans, however, were to be crammed 480 to a carriage and served by a tiny cafeteria.

. . .

In 1992, Malcolm Rifkind, then Transport Secretary, returned to London after riding the Swiss railway network, where he discovered that in the previous year not a single Swiss passenger train had broken down, been cancelled or delayed due to 'staff shortages'.

As if that wasn't galling enough, more than 90 per cent of trains left and arrived within five minutes of their scheduled times. Mr Rifkind was also told that the average Swiss makes 38 rail journeys per year, while his British counterpart makes just 13.

The Toronto Transit Commission built romance into the structure of their new underground system by installing kissing bays in suburban stations. The Commission said: 'We figure most commuters will be driven by their wives in the family car. From stopwatch tests, it takes the average husband 43 seconds to kiss his wife in the car, pick up his case, hat, gloves, get out and close the door. Another three or four seconds can be added if the wife waves goodbye and a further 10 or 15 seconds if there is a pre-school child in the car who also has to be kissed.' Multiply the kissing time by the hundreds of cars arriving at the station during the rush-hour and the answer is utter chaos.

The Commission insists that the kissing bays, where wives can pull off the road to let the husband out without snarling up the traffic behind, will be the best solution to the problem. A spokesman commented: 'You might call them kiss 'n' ride facilities. The idea behind it is to persuade as many people as possible to keep their cars out of the city. And the wife also gets the family car every day.'

. . .

A few years ago, the country's oil difficulties forced the Irish Transport Company to investigate other means of powering trains. Some initial experiments using turf-driven engines proved successful, so plans were made to construct some turf-fired locomotives. Scandinavian engineers expressed considerable interest in the idea.

8

Commuting as Therapy

MANY COMMUTERS AROUND the world describe how trains, in particular, help them to relax. Those commuting heroes who oversleep and end up in distant towns or even foreign countries usually cite the rhythm of the train's wheels as what sent them to sleep. There is indeed evidence of all sorts to suggest that commuting can be . . . well, good for you. But judge for yourself.

. . .

A survey published in New York listed public transport as one of the top ten places where Americans first meet their partners. This disclosure was greeted with some scepticism, considering the state of New York's public transport system. There was even a suggestion that the survey would be developed into a motion picture called *I Married My Mugger*.

. . .

The Hon. Francesco Saverio d'Ayala, 93, spent the last 20 years of his life changing trains. The once rich and successful Italian MP, who was also a distinguished lawyer and diplomat in London, had received a travel permit when he first entered Parliament.

As the years passed, so did the size of his savings, and Francesco was left with only his train pass. Not one to be beaten, Francesco used the free pass to ride up and down the country, making friends and practising his six languages on tourists.

When he died at Turin station, it was estimated that he had clocked up 5 million miles on Italian rails.

· · ·

Italian railworker Luigi Massa found a bizarre method of curing his nervous insomnia – by letting trains run over him. The result was so efficacious that 57-year-old Luigi threw away his sleeping pills and got by on one 'train treatment' every six months. Even Luigi's doctor knew about and approved the revolutionary remedy.

Luigi discovered the calming effects of being underneath a moving train when he was accidentally trapped in front of an express. Like all railworkers, he knew what to do. He simply lay still, parallel to the rails with his head on one side and his feet facing the oncoming train.

His reaction to his predicament was not one of terror but of deep calm, and soon after, his sleeping problem abated. Putting two and two together, Luigi concluded that being run over by a train somehow aided his sleep. His doctor suggested that the deep calm was a form of hypnosis induced by the tremendous noise and rhythm of the train, so Luigi used to sneak off to the tracks during the night to top up his treatment.

One day, however, he went for some daytime therapy and lay down on the track as the Milan–Genoa express thundered towards him at 90 m.p.h. The horrified driver saw the prone body on the line and braked frantically, but too late. The train shot over the body and screeched to a halt. The poor driver was even more horrified when Luigi clambered up from the sleepers and rebuked him for spoiling his treatment.

After a long interrogation by the police, Luigi was allowed to go home. He was feeling very calm. The driver of the train, however, was still in a state of shock.

. . .

Three-year-old Marcos Gonclaves, from Curbita, Brazil, lived near a railway station, where he was told by railway workers that Santa Claus would bring him a real train for Christmas. Marcos woke up early on Christmas Day, saw an empty engine standing on the track and thought it was his present from Santa. He climbed on board and drove it 24 miles.

. . .

A group of soldiers in Hunan, China, fought a fire in a train carrying a load of insecticide while quoting from *The Thoughts of Mao*. Among the heroic deeds of the day, one soldier in particular was singled out. This man stayed calm while his trousers were on fire by reciting the quotation: 'Be resolute; do not fear sacrifice.' He finally had to be taken away, all the while still reciting 'Be resolute . . .'.

. . .

The car-makers Volvo financed extensive research into safe driving. Evidence proved that men would be safer drivers in cold weather if they took their trousers off.

Apparently trousers act as a barrier against conventional methods of car heating, so male drivers turn the heat up to get their legs warm, become drowsy and are therefore in more danger of crashing.

This conclusion came after work done by David P. Wyon with a dummy called Voltman, who was placed in the front seat. Heating was then turned up and the passage of warm air traced through the car. The air in Voltman's trouser leg remained comparatively cool.

. . .

A West German priest compiled his own version of the Ten Commandments for those in traffic jams.

Father Georg Schrami, 33, who himself drives

his Audi 9,000 miles a year round his town in Bavaria, said: 'Many people don't come to church on Sunday because they would rather go for a drive in the country. My book should give them something to think about and encourage them to drive like Christians.'

The book sold out as fast as it was printed. According to Father Schrami, thou shalt not:

Lose thy temper at traffic lights – use the time for a chat with God.

Drive too fast – every time you get the urge, say 'Restrain me, Lord, from putting my foot hard on the accelerator.'

Get mad when looking for somewhere to park – Oh Lord there is nothing more annoying. But God gave me healthy legs – it doesn't hurt to walk a few yards.

. . .

British motorists were also invited to cleanse their souls on Sunday during a drive-in service at a supermarket car park in Warwickshire.

Canon Guy Cornwall-Jones gave a sermon based on the Highway Code, and led drivers in the hymns and a special driver's prayer. Drivers stood by their parked cars throughout the service.

The Canon finished off with a special blessing for the cars and forgiveness for the drivers' motoring sins. He said: 'There seems to be a lot of aggression, fear and emotion in driving these days. We need to bring God back into driving.'

The Canon also planned to play a tape recording of a road accident to shock his parked congregation into driving with more care.

· · ·

A German transport minister, Juergen Warnke, claimed that fast drivers are lousy lovers. Sex problems are one of the main reasons for speeding, he told the transport committee in Bonn. Psychologists report that husbands who don't satisfy their wives tend to try to prove their virility at the wheel. Where all this leaves the drivers of Reliant Robins, we cannot speculate.

· · ·

One Mr Carter from Tottenham sent the following account of his therapeutic driving escapade to a newspaper: 'The other day I parked my car on a meter and found it faulty. Seeing the next one along was working, I popped in a £1 coin. But as I made my way back to the car to move it on to the working meter, someone else zipped in and took my place.

'I attempted to remonstrate with the driver, thinking he would understand the rights of my case. He did not, assuming that possession was nine-tenths of the law. An argument ensued, which resulted in him storming off and me looking for a police officer. This proved unsuccessful.

'I returned to move my car, fearing I might be

clamped. Then I noticed that the driver, in the confusion of events, had left his window open. I slipped my hand in and released the hand brake, pushing the car on to a double yellow line.

'When I returned, I discovered that he had been clamped. I drove off merrily, believing justice had been done.'

. . .

The novelist Brian Freemantle, a daily traveller from Southampton and back, used the time to write eight to nine thousand words each week. Putting all these thousands of words together, he turned them into a novel which turned out to be a best-selling thriller called *Goodbye to an Old Friend*. John le Carré's *The Spy Who Came in from the Cold* was also largely written on the train. Leslie Thomas, the author of *Tropic of Ruislip*, tells of one woman from that town who was so concerned at being associated with a book about urban erotica that she stopped asking for a ticket to Ruislip. Instead, when she returned from London every day, she would ask for Eastcote and pay the extra on arrival.

. . .

While their fellow passengers pen novels, a certain group of commuters on the Waterloo–Southampton line has a fresh round every time the train passes a station beginning with a 'W'. There's

Waterloo for starters, then Wimbledon, Walton, Weybridge, West Byfleet, Woking, Winchfield, Winchester, and still they are nowhere near. Er . . . now where exactly were they going?

. . .

A commuter who wants to remain anonymous for the sake of his marriage once went for A Quick One After Work and fell asleep on the train. Missing his stop at Peterborough, he woke at Doncaster at 10.40 p.m. When he asked the time of the next train homewards, he was told it was not until 1.30 a.m.

He realized that it was now 4 hours since he had left his office local, and the prospect of spending another 3 hours on Doncaster station without some liquid sustenance was not a cheery prospect, so asked if there was a pub nearby. 'Pubs are shut but there's a night club round t'corner,' said a helpful ticket collector.

Five minutes later he was in 'Seventh Heaven' looking a little out of place in his suit and raincoat among local miners on a night out, but being welcomed in a big way by the local girls. 'It was one of the best nights I've ever had,' he later — much later — declared, 'and I still caught the 1.30 a.m. home.'